Succeed on the NJ A

This Book Includes:

- •4 NJ ASK Practice tests similar to the actual test
- •Detailed answer explanations for every question
- •In-depth coverage of multiple-choice and open-ended questions
- •Strategies for building speed and accuracy

Plus One Year access to Online Workbooks

- •Hundreds of practice questions
- •Individualized score reports
- •Instant feedback after completion of the workbook
- •Students can complete the Online Workbooks at their own pace

Complement Classroom Learning All Year

Using the Lumos Study Program, parents and teachers can reinforce the classroom learning experience for children. It creates a collaborative learning platform for students, teachers and parents.

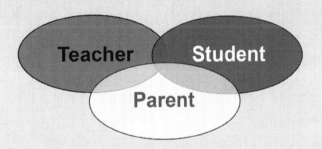

Lumos Study Program is Used by Leading New Jersey Libraries

Lumos Learning

NJ ASK Practice Tests and Online Workbooks: Language Arts Literacy Grade 4, Second Edition

Contributing Editor	- Jodi Kaspin
Contributing Editor	- Natalie Thau
Project Direcotr	- Sharmila Krishnaswamy
Repository Administrator	- Shyam Panyam
Designer and Illustrator	- Mirona Jova

ISBN: 9781442105850

Printed in the United States of America

For permissions and additional information contact us

Lumos Information Services, LLC
PO Box 1575, Piscataway, NJ 08855-1575
http://www.lumostestprep.com

Email: support@lumostestprep.com
Tel: (732) 384-0146
Fax: (866)283-6471

Lumos Learning

Table of Contents

Introduction

The New Jersey Assessment of Skills and Knowledge (NJ ASK) is a comprehensive standards-based assessment administered in the New Jersey schools every year. Student success on this test has significant benefits to all stake holders – students, parents, teachers, and school administration. Success on this test requires students to demonstrate good test taking skills and competency in all key areas covered in the New Jersey Core Curriculum Content Standards.

How can students succeed on the NJ ASK through this Lumos Study Program?
At Lumos Learning, we believe that yearlong learning and adequate practice before the actual test are the keys to student success on the NJ ASK. We have designed the Lumos NJ ASK Study Program to help students get plenty of realistic practice before the test and to promote yearlong collaborative learning.

Inside this book, you will find **four full-length practice tests** that are similar to the NJ ASK. Completing these tests will help students master the different areas that are included in the New Jersey Core Curriculum Standards and practice test taking skills. The results will help the students and educators get insights into students' strengths and weaknesses in particular content areas. These insights could be used to help students strengthen their skills in difficult topics and to improve speed and accuracy while taking the test.

The Lumos NJ ASK **Online Workbooks** are designed to promote yearlong learning. It is a simple program students can access using a computer with internet access in a secure manner. It consists of hundreds of grade appropriate questions based on the New Jersey Core Curriculum Content Standards. Students will get instant feedback and can review their answers anytime. Each student's answers and progress can be reviewed by parents and educators to reinforce the learning experience.

How to use this book effectively

The Lumos NJ ASK Study Program is a flexible learning tool. It can be adapted to suit a student's skill level and the time available to practice before the NJ ASK. Here are some tips to help you use this book and the online workbooks effectively:

Students
- You can use the "Diagnostic Test" to understand your mastery of different topics and test taking skills.
- Use the "Related Lumos Online Workbook" in the Answer Key section to identify the topic that is related to each question.
- Use the Online workbooks to practice your areas of difficulty and complement class room learning.
- Have open-ended responses evaluated by a teacher or parent keeping in mind the scoring rubrics.
- Take the "Practice Tests" as you get close to the NJ ASK test date.
- Complete the test in a quiet place, following the test guidelines. Practice tests provide you an opportunity to improve your test taking skills and to review topics included in the NJ ASK test.

Parents
- Familiarize yourself with the test format and expectations.
- Help your child use Lumos Online Workbooks by following the instructions in "How to access the Lumos Online Workbooks" section of this chapter.
- Review your child's performance in the "Lumos Online Workbooks" periodically. You can do this by simply asking your child to log into the system online and selecting the subject area you wish to review.

Review your child's work in the Practice Tests. To get a sense of how the open-ended questions are graded review scoring rubrics online at http://www.state.nj.us/education/assessment/es

Teacher/Tutors
- You can use the Online Workbooks to complement your classroom training.

If you are using this program with several children, please contact support@lumostestprep.com and request a teacher account. This will help you review the work of all your students efficiently.

LumosTestPrep.com

NJ ASK Frequently Asked Questions

What is the NJ ASK?

It is an assessment based on the New Jersey Core Curriculum Content Standards. It is administered in all New Jersey public schools. With the enactment of the No Child Left Behind Act, it is administered every year to all children in grade 3 through 8. Students in Grade 4 are tested in Mathematics, Science and Language Arts Literacy. NJ ASK scores are reported as scale scores in each content area. The scores range from 100-199 (Partially Proficient), 200-249 (Proficient) and 250-300 (Advanced Proficient).

When is the NJ ASK given?

It is normally administered in the spring. Please obtain the exact dates of your test from your school.

What is the format of the NJ ASK?

The NJ ASK consists of multiple choice and open-ended questions for the Reading tasks and Writing tasks. In multiple choice questions, students are expected to select the best answer out of four choices.

For open-ended questions, students are asked to construct written responses, in their own words. For the writing tasks a writing situation will be given and questions will asked accordingly. The students are expected to write an answer in their own words. Each test section needs to be completed in the allotted time. Test administrators ensure that students adhere to the test guidelines.

What is the duration of the test?

Grade 4 students take the NJ ASK over a five day period. The first two days are devoted to the Language Arts Literacy test. The next two days to Mathematics test and the final day to the science test. On each of the test days students spend from 60 to 100 minutes working on the test.

Where can I get additional information about the NJ ASK?

You can obtain a lot of useful information about the test, schedules and performance reports by visiting the New Jersey State Department of Education's website at
http://www.state.nj.us/education/assessment/

How to access the Lumos Online Workbooks

First Time Access:

Using a computer with internet access, go to
http://www.lumostestprep.com/book

Select the name of your book from the book selection drop-down menu.

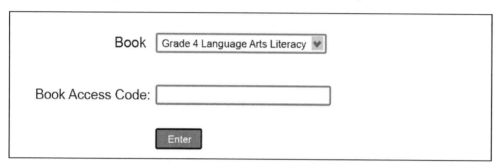

Enter the following access code in the Access Code field and press the Enter button.
Access Code: 5323202890

In the next screen, click on the "New User" button to register your user name and password.

Welcome NJ ASK Grade 4 Language Arts Literacy
Book Customer!

If you are a New User, please register.

Login

Password

Enter

Subsequent Access:

After you establish your user id and password for subsequent access, simply login with your account information.

What if I buy more than one Lumos Study Program?

Please note that you can access all Online Workbooks using one user id and password. If you buy more than one Lumos Study Program book, simply follow the instruction above for First Time Access for the first book. Please work on one work book before you exit.

Go back to the http://www.lumostestprep.com/book link and select the second book from the book selection drop-down menu. Enter the access code in the Access Code field provided in the second book. In the next screen simply login using your previously created account.

LumosTestPrep.com

Test Taking Tips

1) **The day before the test**, make sure you get a good night's sleep.
2) **On the day of the test**, be sure to eat a good hearty breakfast! Also, be sure to arrive at school on-time.
3) **During the test:**

> Read every question carefully.
> While Answering Multiple-Choice questions:
>> • Do not circle the answer choices. Fill in the bubble corresponding to your answer choice.
>> • Read **all** of the answer choices, even if think you have found the correct answer.
>> • Do not spend too much time on any one question. Work steadily through all questions in the section.
>> • Attempt all of the questions even if you are not sure of some answers.
>> • If you run into a difficult question, eliminate as many choices as you can and then pick the best one of the remaining choices. Intelligent guessing will help you increase your score.
>> • Also, mark the question so that if you have extra time, you can return to it after you reach the end of the section. Try to erase the marks after you complete the work.
>> • Some questions may refer to a graph, chart, or other kind of picture. Carefully review the graphic before answering the question.
>
> While Answering Open-ended questions:
>> • Open-ended questions typically have multiple parts. Make sure you answer **all** parts clearly.
>> • Be sure to include explanations for your written responses and show all work.
>> • Some questions may refer to a graph, chart, or other kind of picture. Carefully review the graphic before answering the question.

Good Luck!!

Diagnostic Test

Student Name: _____   Start Time: _____
Test Date: _____   End Time: _____

Writing Task 1

Johnny was a fourth grader. He was known as "the problem solver". One day, his neighbor's cat was acting unusually aggressive. Johnny figured out that the cat was acting that way because he had a thorn in his foot.

Now discuss a time when you solved a problem involving a friend, family member or someone close to you. Describe what the problem was and explain how you resolved it?

•You may take notes, create a web, or do other prewriting work in the space provided. Then, write your story on the lines provided.

•After you complete writing your composition, read what you have written. Make sure that your writing is the best it can be.

Prewriting Area

Writing Task 1

LumosTestPrep.com

Reading Task 1

Directions to the Student

Now you will read a story and answer the questions that follow.
Some questions will be multiple-choice; others will be open-ended.

- You may look back at the reading passage as often as you want.
- Read each question carefully and think about the answer and fill in the circle completely next to your choice.
- If you do not know the answer to a question, go on to the next question and come back to the skipped question later.

LumosTestPrep.com

Jeremy's swimming championship
By Jodi-Anne Kaspin

"On your mark..." Jeremy stood in position, ready for his dive. "Get set..." His heart was beating so fast, it felt like it would pop out. "Go!" Jeremy heard the gun go off as the water splashed over his head and his entire body.

This was the championship — the day he was waiting for since the beginning of the swimming season. His friends and him have been talking about this day since he can remember! They've been training two hours a day, eating well, stretching as much as they could... all for this!

Jeremy entered the water and felt like he was in his own world. While underwater those first few seconds, he barely heard the world above him. He started his kicking and slow-ly came up to the surface. All of a sudden, the sounds from the audience engulfed him! Jeremy found that the voices sounded like they were one loud voice, cheering him on as if this race determined his future! He picked his arms out of the water and pulled them back as quickly as he could. At the same time, his legs were swiftly moving through the water.

As he was moving, he thought about why this meant more to him than anyone else on his team. He thought about how long it took to get over his serious illness and how he expected that he time he lost would never allow him to return to the water this year... or even in years to come. Jeremy sat in that hospital for months on end, just thinking, and wanting to be in the position he is in right now. It almost feels like a miracle.

"Go! Go! Go! Go!" Jeremy continued to swim his hardest and tried to act as a fish pounding through the water. He looked to his right and saw an empty lane. Where was his opponent? Was he ahead or was he behind Jeremy? He couldn't know for sure.

His mind went trailing back to his days in the hospital. His teammates were so helpful, so cooperative, and so enthusiastic. He felt so depressed lying in that bed for so long and his teammates just stood by his side and tried to entertain him in their free time. He really had such incredible friends.

His arms were pushing through the water as he took advantage of the few breaths he could take. Just keep on going, Jeremy told himself. Just keep on going! Just a few more laps left of freestyle stroke! He looked beside him and he saw some splashing. "Is this my competition?" he asked himself. "Can I try to beat them?" He didn't want to let his teammates down. They were so close to winning this meet. The place he came in would depend on the winning of his team.

Jeremy tried to think positive even though his heart was beating and he was starting to feel a slight cramp in his side. He shouldn't have enjoyed that third piece of pizza during lunch, he lectured to himself. In order to make the time go by, he remembered what his mom suggested: sing his favorite song in his mind until his last two laps. Jeremy thought maybe his mom was right—it might keep his mind off the stressful situation.

The song was working! The time seemed to fly as he continued his pattern. Just stroke, stroke, stroke, and breathe.

  LumosTestPrep.com

Three strokes and then breathe. Jeremy even forgot for a split second where he was since he was concentrating so much on this song in his head. Finally, the gun went off in the background, meaning it's the final lap of the race. Only one more left!

He gave it all he had. Jeremy forgot about the song, and thought about how much this race means to him, his family, and his teammates. He barely took any breaths as he started to view the wall right ahead. It was almost there…

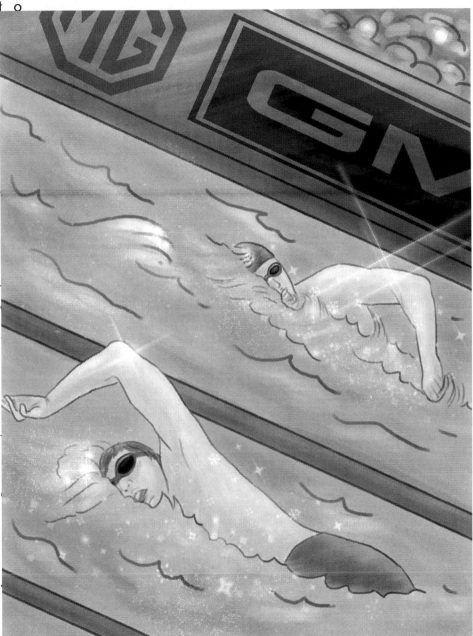

Finally, his two hands touched the wall. Jeremy was afraid to look up. he did, he would have face the results of the race. If he just stayed down in the water, he was fine, right? He knew what he had do. His head popped of the water and he heard the cheering the background. He looked to the right, and there was no one there. Good so far! Then he checked to left of him, and saw a competitor already with goggles off and getting of the pool. He realized came in second, and first reaction was to be angry with himself. Jeremy needed this to help the team! They were going to be so disappointed.

Yet, to his surprise, there were several of his teammates coming toward him. Actually, he realized they were running towards him. "But why?" Jeremy asked himself. "I didn't get the points we needed," he thought.

Before he could say a word, his friends wrapped their arms around him, giving him words of praise and support. In fact, he looked around and it looked like the audience was giving him a standing ovation!

He was overwhelmed with so much emotion. It turns out that the team was more concerned with him finishing his race due to his time out of the water that they didn't care about how he did. The fact that he was healthy was all that mattered to anyone. Tears began to flow down Jeremy's cheek.

   LumosTestPrep.com

1. What types of writing would this passage be considered?

   Ⓐ   nonfiction
   Ⓑ   fables
   Ⓒ   realistic fiction
   Ⓓ   scientific fiction

2. Based on Jeremy's thoughts in the passage, what do you think affected Jeremy the most when swimming to win?

   Ⓐ   His illness
   Ⓑ   Helping his teammates
   Ⓒ   His family
   Ⓓ   His training

3. Based on the passage, what do you think engulfed means?

   Ⓐ   To overwhelm someone
   Ⓑ   To sing to
   Ⓒ   To yell at
   Ⓓ   To jump on

4. What were some successful techniques that Jeremy used to keep his mind off the race?

   Ⓐ   Think about his teammates support and sing to himself
   Ⓑ   Sing to himself and kick very hard
   Ⓒ   Dive his favorite dive and swim underwater as long as he can
   Ⓓ   Work with his coach privately to learn how to make himself better

5. How did the author explain what had happened to Jeremy in the past?

   Ⓐ   Jeremy told the readers
   Ⓑ   His friends explain to the readers
   Ⓒ   The author switched the setting during the race to tell of the past
   Ⓓ   None of these

6. Which of the following sentences explain the main idea of the above story?

   Ⓐ   Winning is the most important thing in a race.
   Ⓑ   Completing the race without giving up no matter what happens is more important than winning the race.
   Ⓒ   It is ok to give up without giving it your best.
   Ⓓ   None of these

It turns out that the team was more concerned with him finishing his race due to his time out of the water that they didn't care about how he did.

7. What is the meaning of the above sentence?

Ⓐ Jeremy's friends did not care about him much.
Ⓑ The team was more concerned about winning than Jeremy
Ⓒ The team was proud of Jeremy that he finished the race even though he was sick for so long.
Ⓓ The team did not care about winning.

8. According to the above passage Jeremy was a _____.

Ⓐ Scuba Diver
Ⓑ Life guard
Ⓒ Swim teacher
Ⓓ Athlete

Tears began to flow down Jeremy's cheek.

9. Why did Jeremy have tears?

Ⓐ because he was crying
Ⓑ because he had allergies
Ⓒ because he lost the race
Ⓓ because he was overwhelmed with emotion

10. **The passage above is about a boy named Jeremy who tries his best to win a swimming championship.**

   - **Discuss Jeremy's situation in your own words.**
   - **Describe if you think Jeremy should have won the race in the story.**
   - **Explain why or why not.**

LumosTestPrep.com

Writing Task 2
Directions to the Student

Read the poem "Wind". After you are done, you will do a writing task. The poem may give you ideas for your writing.

Wind

Wind, come softly.
Don't break the shutters of the windows.
Don't scatter the papers.
Don't throw down the books on the shelf.
There, look what you did — you threw them all down.
You tore the pages of the books.
You brought rain again.
You're very clever at poking fun at weaklings.
Frail crumbling houses, crumbling doors, crumbling rafters,
crumbling wood, crumbling bodies, crumbling lives,
crumbling hearts —
The wind breaks windows and crushes them all.
He won't do what you tell him.
So, come, let's build strong homes,
Let's joint the doors firmly.
Practice to firm the body.
Make the heart steadfast.
Do this, and the wind will be friends with us.
The wind blows out weak fires.
He makes strong fires roar and flourish.
His friendship is good.
We praise him every day.
- by Subramaniya Bharati. Translated by A.K. Ramanujan

Writing Task 2

The poem "Wind" praises all that the wind does for us.

- **Discuss whether or not you agree with the poem.**
- **Describe why you agree or disagree.**
- **Explain what we can do to help protect ourselves from the wind.**

- You may take notes, create a web, or do other prewriting work. Then, write your composition on the lines provided.
- After you finish writing your composition, carefully read what you have written and make sure that your writing is the best it can be.

Prewriting Area

Writing Task 2

LumosTestPrep.com

Reading Task 2

Directions to the Student

Now you will read another passage and answer the questions that follow. Some questions will be multiple-choice; others will be open-ended.

- You may look back at the reading passage as often as you want.
- Read each question carefully and think about the answer and fill in the circle completely next to your choice.
- If you do not know the answer to a question, go on to the next question and come back to the skipped question later.

LumosTestPrep.com

Benjamin Franklin

Excerpts from ushistory.org

Benjamin Franklin is a huge part of American History.

During his more than 80 years of life, this intelligent man made such a difference in the lives of not only the American colonists who lived at the end of the 1700's, but in our lives today! Not only was Benjamin Franklin an important part of the American Revolution, he also contributed a vast amount of inventions that helped the American colonists during the 1700's.

He was a writer, a scientist, a leader, and an inventor and used his talents to create new products that we still use to-day!

Benjamin Franklin was born in Boston on January 17, 1706. He was the tenth son of soap maker named Josiah Franklin.

Benjamin's mother was Abiah Folger, the second wife of Josiah. In all, Josiah would have 17 children! That means Benjamin would have 16 siblings!

Josiah wanted for Benjamin to join the clergy. However, Josiah could only afford to send his son to school for one year and clergymen needed years of education. But, as young Benjamin loved to read, his father had him apprenticed by his brother James, who was a printer. After helping James compose pamphlets, 12-year-old Benjamin would sell their products in the streets.

When Benjamin was 15, his brother started The New England Courant, the first newspaper in Boston. The paper contained articles, opinion pieces written by James's friends, advertisements, and ship schedules.

As he became a little older, Benjamin Franklin was concerned with getting information out to the public. In 1732, he created Poor Richard's Almanac, which was published annually to give people information on various subjects and gave advice to people. One of the pieces of advice were "there are no pains without gains," which means that people don't gain anything unless they put forth effort. Benjamin Franklin's almanac was very popular and sold many copies.

Ben Franklin had poor vision and needed glasses for both near and far throughout his life. Rather than continue to take on and off his two pairs of glasses, he thought of a way to create one pair that does the job of both types of glasses. He created what we know today as bifocals, which help people to see both near and far.

Another one of Benjamin Franklin's inventions included the Franklin Stove. During colonial times, colonists would build fires in their homes in order help keep their families warm from the vicious winters that took place. Since this method proved to be dangerous, Benjamin Franklin invented the stove that would heat entire homes without the risk of causing fires. He also started the first fire department so the citizens in Philadelphia could feel safe and protected.

As a postman, Ben Franklin wanted to figure out how many miles he rode in between his routes. As a result, he invented a simple odometer and put it on his carriage.

Benjamin Franklin has such a great involvement in society as we know it today. Thanks to this brilliant man, we have so many more opportunities in our lives. He is not only remembered as a leader in the independence of the United States, but as an outstanding inventor of many useful creations.

11. Why do you think the author wrote the passage?

Ⓐ to tell about Benjamin Franklin's life
Ⓑ to determine why the American colonists wanted independence
Ⓒ to explain why Benjamin Franklin was important in history
Ⓓ to describe Benjamin Franklin's inventions and why they were important

12. Based on the passage, what do you think is an odometer?

Ⓐ a part of a carriage
Ⓑ an object to measure the amount of miles
Ⓒ a letter that needs to be mailed
Ⓓ none of these

13. What was the order of the inventions listed in the passage?

Ⓐ lightning rod, library, bifocals, fire department, odometer
Ⓑ odometer, library, bifocals, fire department, almanac
Ⓒ almanac, bifocals, stove, fire department, odometer
Ⓓ none of these

14. Which was NOT an invention mentioned in the passage?

Ⓐ lightning rod
Ⓑ fire department
Ⓒ bifocal glasses
Ⓓ they were all mentioned in the story

15. What do you think vast means?

Ⓐ helpful
Ⓑ large
Ⓒ colonial
Ⓓ a long time ago

16. According to the above passage Benjamin Franklin was born in _____ city.

Ⓐ Boston
Ⓑ Massachusetts
Ⓒ Philadelphia
Ⓓ New England

17. Who were Benjamin Franklin's parents?

Ⓐ Soap sellers and revolutionists
Ⓑ Josiah Franklin and Abiah Folger
Ⓒ The clergy
Ⓓ None of these

18. Who was Benjamin Franklin?

Ⓐ He was an Inventor and a teacher
Ⓑ He was a leader and a soap maker
Ⓒ He was a leader, a scientist, a writer and an inventor
Ⓓ He was a professor and a teacher

19. According to the above passage Benjamin Franklin live in the _____.

Ⓐ 1500
Ⓑ 1600
Ⓒ 1800
Ⓓ 1700

20. The passage above talks about Benjamin Franklin's inventions.

- Discuss some inventions that Benjamin Franklin created.
- Describe some of his inventions that effect YOU today.
- Explain how they help you.

   LumosTestPrep.com

Reading Task 3

Directions to the Student

Now you will read a story and answer the questions that follow.
Some questions will be multiple-choice; others will be open-ended.

- You may look back at the reading passage as often as you want.
- Read each question carefully and think about the answer and fill in the circle completely next to your choice.
- If you do not know the answer to a question, go on to the next question and come back to the skipped question later.

The Needle
By Hans Christian Andersen

There was once a needle, which thought her so fine; she imagined she was an embroidering-needle.

"Take care, and mind you hold me tight!" she said to the Fingers that took her out. "Don't let me fall! If I fall on the ground I shall certainly never be found again, for I am so fine!"

"That's as it may be," said the Fingers; and they grasped her round.

"See, I'm coming with a train!" said the needle, and she drew a long thread after her, but

there was no knot in the thread.

The Fingers pointed the needle just at the cook's slipper, in which the upper leather had burst, and was to be sewn together.

"That's too tough," said the needle. "I shall never get through. I'm breaking! I'm breaking!" And she really broke. "Did I not say so?" said the needle; "I'm too fine!"

     LumosTestPrep.com

"Now it's quite useless," said the Fingers; but they were obliged to hold her fast, all the same; for the cook dropped some sealing wax upon the needle, and pinned her handkerchief together with it in front.

"So, now I'm a breast-pin!" said the needle. "I knew very well that I should come to honor; when one is something, one comes to something!"

And she laughed quietly to herself—and one can never see when a needle laughs. There she sat, as proud as if she were in a state coach, and looked all about her.

"May I be permitted to ask if you are of gold?" she inquired of the pin, her neighbor. "You have a very pretty appearance and a peculiar head, but it is only little. You must take pains to grow, for it's not every one that has sealing-wax dropped upon him."

And the needle drew her self up so proudly that she fell out of the handkerchief right into the sink, which the cook was rinsing out.

"Now we're going on a journey," said the needle. "If I only don't get lost!"

But she really was lost.

"I'm too fine for this world," she observed, as she lay in the gutter. "But I know who I am, and there's always something in that!"

So the needle kept her proud behavior, and did not lose her good humor. And things of many kinds swam over her, chips and straws and pieces of old newspapers.

"Only look how they sail!" said the needle. "They don't know what is under them! I'm here, I remain firmly here. See, there goes a chip thinking of nothing in the world but of himself—of a chip! There's a straw going by now. How he turns! How he twirls about! Don't think only of yourself, you might easily run up against a stone.

There swims a bit of newspaper. What's written upon it has long been forgotten, and yet it gives itself airs. I sit quietly and patiently here. I know who I am, and I shall remain what I am."

One day something lay close beside her that glittered splendidly; then the needle believed that it was a diamond; but it was a bit of broken bottle; and because it shone the needle spoke to it, introducing herself as a breastpin.

"I suppose you are a diamond?" she observed.

"Why, yes, something of that kind."

And then each believed the other to be a very valuable thing; and they began speaking about the world, and how very conceited it was.

"I have been in a lady's box," said the needle, "and this lady was a cook. She had five fingers on each hand, and I never saw anything so conceited as those five fingers. And yet they were only there that they might take me out of the box and put me back into it."

"There were five brothers, all of the finger family. They kept very proudly together though they were of different lengths: the outermost, the thumbling, was short and fat; he walked out in front of the ranks, and only had one joint in his back, and could only make a single bow; but he said that if he were hacked off a man, that man was useless for service in war. Dainty-mouth, the second finger, thrust himself into sweet and sour, pointed to sun and moon, and gave the impression when they wrote. Longman, the third, looked at all the others over his shoulder. Goldborder, the fourth, went about with a golden belt round his waist; and little Playman did nothing at all, and was proud of it. There was nothing but bragging among them, and therefore I went away."

"And now we sit here and glitter!" said the Bit of Bottle.

At that moment more water came into the gutter, so that it overflowed, and the Bit of Bottle was carried away.

"So he is disposed of," observed the needle. "I remain here. I am too fine. But that's my pride, and my pride is honorable." And proudly she sat there, and had many great thoughts. "I could almost believe I had been born of a sunbeam, I'm so fine! It really appears as if the sunbeams were always seeking for me under the water. Ah! I'm so fine that my mother cannot find me. If I had my old eye, which broke off, I think I should cry; but, no, I should not do that; it's not genteel to cry."

One day a couple of street boys lay grubbing in the gutter, where they sometimes found old nails, farthings, and similar treasures. It was dirty work, but they took great delight in it.

"Oh!" cried one, who had pricked himself with the needle, "there's a fellow for you!"

"I'm not a fellow; I'm a young lady!" said the needle.

But nobody listened to her. The sealing wax had come off, and she had turned black; but black makes one look slender, and she thought herself finer even than before.

"Here comes an eggshell sailing along!" said the boys; and they stuck the needle fast in the eggshell.

"White walls, and black myself! That looks well," remarked the needle. "Now one can see me. I only hope I shall not be seasick!" But she was not seasick at all. "It is good against seasickness, if one has a steel stomach, and does not forget that one is a little more than an ordinary person! Now my seasickness is over. The finer one is, the more one can bear."

"Crack!" went the eggshell, for a wagon went over her.

"Good Heavens, how it crushes one!" said the needle. "I'm getting seasick now—I'm quite sick."

But she was not really sick, though the wagon went over her; she lay there at full length, and there she may lie.

LumosTestPrep.com

21. Who are "Dainty-Mouth" and "Goldborder?"

Ⓐ Other needles
Ⓑ The second finger and the fourth finger
Ⓒ The pinky finger and the thumb
Ⓓ Two pieces of glass

22. What would be a best adjective to describe the needle?

Ⓐ Proud
Ⓑ Silly
Ⓒ Huge
Ⓓ Argumentative

23. What did the needle think she was going to do when she said "I only hope I shall not be seasick"?

Ⓐ She thought she was going to drink water
Ⓑ She thought she was going to dive in the bathtub
Ⓒ She thought she was going to float in the eggshell
Ⓓ None of these

24. Why did the needle think the broken glass was a diamond?

Ⓐ It looked like a diamond
Ⓑ She was told it was a diamond
Ⓒ It was shiny just like a diamond
Ⓓ It said "diamond" on it

25. What type of story would this be considered?

Ⓐ Fairy tale
Ⓑ Realistic fiction
Ⓒ Poetry
Ⓓ Science fiction

26. Who is the little Playman?

Ⓐ Thumb
Ⓑ Middle finger
Ⓒ A Violinist
Ⓓ Little finger

The Fingers pointed the needle just at the cook's slipper, in which the upper leather had burst, and was to be sewn together.

27. According to the above sentence what was needle used for?

    Ⓐ To do embroidery
    Ⓑ To sew a leather bag
    Ⓒ To sew the cook's dress
    Ⓓ To sew the cooks leather slipper.

28. According to the above passage how did the needle get in the gutter?

    Ⓐ The cook threw it in to the gutter
    Ⓑ The needle fell in to the sink where the cook was washing and was washed into the gutter
    Ⓒ The needle just fell into the gutter
    Ⓓ It was always lying in the gutter

29.   What happened to the needle in the end?

    Ⓐ It was picked up by a couple of street boys
    Ⓑ It got washed away in the gutter
    Ⓒ It sailed away in the eggshell
    Ⓓ It lay on the ground even after a wagon went over her

    LumosTestPrep.com

Here are some reminders for completing this Open-Ended task:

- Focus your response on the question asked.
- Answer all parts of the question and explain your answer with specific details.
- Use specific information from the story to answer all the parts of the question

30. **The story above talks about a needle that travels to different places.**

- **Discuss where the needle travels.**
- **Describe where you think the needle is right now.**
- **Explain your answer above.**

End Of Diagnostic Test

     LumosTestPrep.com

Diagnostic Test Answers

Sample Answer for Writing Task 1

A 5-point response should include

- Answers to all parts of the question
- Reference to the text in the response
- Personal comparisons

Everyone experiences problems in their life and sometimes, they are hard to solve. One time in my life when I had a problem like this was when my family and cousins got locked out of the house. That was one of the scariest moments of my life! Here is how it all started.

It was a cold Saturday morning in the winter. My cousins from Tennessee came over for the holidays, and we were planning to treat them with a ski trip. After waking up in the morning, everyone was hustling around; packing food, jackets and ski gears. In the rush, we forgot one major thing. Last night, my mom unhooked the house keys from the van keys to let my cousins come in late in the night without disturbing rest of us. The next morning, she was planning to hook it back to the van keys. But with all the rush in the morning, I guess we forgot to take the house keys!

During the day while we were having the fun skiing, no one realized that we were missing the keys, until we came back late in the night. Everyone was so tired and cold that no one wanted to leave the warm van and explore the options. So my dad and I decided to look around trying to see if we could open the back door. We tried shoving the back door open. Unfortunately, it wouldn't budge. After spending 20 minutes to try different things, we decided to give up and go spend the night at a motel. Before we gave up, I decided to put a little more effort towards getting in. As we were about to leave, an idea popped into my mind. Sometimes, we open the dining room window for fresh air. So chances are that it might be open. We went back again and tried to open the dining room window. Guess what? The window was unlocked and I was able to climb through it.

When my cousins heard of my discovery, they were all happy and excited. We finally found a way to get in. It had been a long day with all the problems that we had. So we were all glad to be back home and everyone were proud of my idea !!!

Reading Task 1 Answer Key

Question No.	Correct Answer
1	C
2	B
3	A
4	A
5	C
6	B
7	C
8	D
9	D

Sample Answer for Open–Ended 1

A 4-point response should include:

- Answer to all parts of the question
- Reference to the text in response
- Personal comparisons

In the story, Jeremy was a very hard worker who loved to swim. He practiced swimming every day and always wanted to do his best for both himself and his team. He strove to be the best he could be! When it came down to the big swimming meet, he was incredibly nervous. He wanted to win the meet for his team and knew that he had to earn first place to do that. I think Jeremy should have won the race because he wanted to win for his team and not just for himself. However, even though Jeremy didn't win, he should have been happy with how well he performed and how hard he tried. His teammates saw his determination and congratulated him for all his hard work.

LumosTestPrep.com

Sample Answer for Writing Task 2

A 5-point response should include:

- Answers to all parts of the question
- Reference to the text in the response
- Personal comparisons

    The poem "Wind" tells a very important message about the wind. Not only does the poem tell about how the wind is harmful, but it also tells how the wind can be helpful. I both agree and disagree with this poem for a few reasons.

    I agree with the poem's message about the harmful effects of the wind. The wind can cause chaos and damage to things like homes, doors and windows. This damage can upset people and destroy important parts of our lives and this is why the wind can hurt us. I also disagree with parts of the poem. It is not really possible to be friends with the wind. The wind is something that happens in nature and is something a person cannot control. Even if we are "friends with the wind" it can still hurt us.

    In order to protect ourselves from the wind, we can take action. We can use certain objects to hold items down that may blow away. When it is windy, we can close the windows to the house so papers don't fly away. We can also use special shutters to keep us safe during very bad storms. These are just some examples of how we can protect ourselves from the wind.

Reading Task 2 Answer Key

Question No.	Correct Answer
11	D
12	B
13	C
14	A
15	B
16	A
17	B
18	C
19	D

Sample Answer for Open-Ended 2

A 4-point response should include:

- Answer to all parts of the question
- Reference to the text in response
- Personal comparisons

Some of the things that Benjamin Franklin invented that were mentioned in the passage are the bifocals, the stove, and the odometer. There are many things that Benjamin Franklin invented that greatly affect me today. The two inventions that affect me the most are the stove and the creation of the first fire department. I love to bake and cook. It is one of my favorite things to do, especially with my mom. If it were not for Benjamin Franklin, I would not be able to bake and cook as easily as I do today. He made it possible for people to live an easier life by providing them with the tools to cook food in a better way. Benjamin Franklin also created the first fire department. It is because of him that we are kept safe from fires. I think Benjamin Franklin was so smart to create this, especially since he invented the stove, which can cause fires if people do not use them carefully.

Reading Task 3 Answer Key

Question No.	Correct Answer
21	B
22	A
23	C
24	C
25	A
26	D
27	D
28	B
29	D

Sample Answer for Open-Ended 3

A 4-point response should include:

- Answer to all parts of the question
- Reference to the text in response
- Personal comparisons

I think the needle is no longer there. I believe the needle got stuck in the wagon wheel and traveled for many miles into the local town. Once it was in town, it eventually fell off the wheel of the wagon. While it was lying on the road, an old woman, who enjoyed knitting for the children in the town orphanage, found the needle. She picked it up and thought to herself, "I am missing my favorite needle. This will be perfect!" She brought the needle back to her house and began knitting for the children. The needle was finally happy because it was no longer lonely. From then on, the needle and old woman spent many long hours together knitting.

Notes

LumosTestPrep.com

Practice Test - 1

Student Name: Start Time:
Test Date: End Time:

Writing Task 1

Most people like to read books. Many of them have favorite authors whose books they like to read most. Who is your favorite author and why? Name this author's best book, and explain why you think it is well written.

- You may take notes, create a web, or do other prewriting work in the space provided. Then, write your story on the lines provided.
- After you complete writing your composition, read what all you have written. Make sure that your writing is the best it can be.

Prewriting Area

LumosTestPrep.com

Writing Task 1

LumosTestPrep.com

Reading Task 1

Directions to the Student

Now you will read a story and answer the questions that follow.
Some questions will be multiple-choice; others will be open-ended.

- You may look back at the reading passage as often as you want.
- Read each question carefully and think about the answer and fill in the circle completely next to your choice.
- If you do not know the answer to a question, go on to the next question and come back to the skipped question later.

The Three Sillies

Adapted by Joseph Jacobs

Once upon a time there was a farmer and his wife who had one daughter, and a gentleman courted her. Every evening he used to come and see her, and stop to supper at the farmhouse, and the daughter used to be sent down into the cellar to draw the juice for supper.

So one evening she had gone down to draw the juice, and she happened to look up at the ceiling while she was drawing, and she saw a mallet stuck in one of the beams. It must have been there a long, long time, but somehow or other she had never noticed it before, and she began a-thinking.

And she thought it was very dangerous to have that mallet there, for she said to herself: "Suppose him and me was to be married, and we was to have a son, and he was to grow up to be a man, and come down into the cellar to get the juice, like as I'm doing now, and the mallet was to fall on his head and kill him, what a dreadful thing it would be!"

And she put down the candle and the jug, and sat herself down and began a-crying.

Well, they began to wonder upstairs how it was that she was so long, and her mother went down to see after her, and she found her sitting on the settle crying, and the juice running over the floor. "Why, whatever is the matter?" said her mother. "Oh, mother!" says she, "look at that horrid mallet! Suppose we was to be married, and was to have a son, and he was to grow up, and was to come down to the cellar, and the mallet was to fall on his head and kill him, what a dreadful thing it would be!"

"Dear, dear! What a dreadful thing it would be!" said the mother, and she sat her down beside the daughter and started crying too. Then after a bit the father began to wonder that they didn't come back, and he went down into the cellar to look for them himself, and there they two sat crying, and the juice running all over the floor. "Whatever is the matter?" says he. "Why," says the mother, "look at that horrid mallet. Just suppose, if our daughter and her sweetheart was to be married, and was to have a son, and he was to grow up, and was to come down into the cellar to draw the beer, and the mallet was to fall on his head and kill him, what a dreadful thing it would be!" "Dear, dear,

dear! So it would!" said the father, and he sat himself down aside of the other two, and started a-crying.

Now the gentleman got tired of stopping up in the kitchen by himself, and at last he went down into the cellar too, to see what they were after; and there they three sat crying side by side, and the juice running all over the floor. And he ran straight to them. Then he said: "Whatever are you three doing, sitting there crying, and letting the juice run all over the floor?" "Oh!" says the father, "look at that horrid mallet! Suppose you and our daughter was to be married, and was to have a son, and he was to grow up, and was to come down into the cellar to draw the beer, and the mallet was to fall on his head and kill him!" And then they all started crying worse than before.

But the gentleman burst out laughing, and reached up and pulled out the mallet, and then he said: "I've traveled many miles, and I never met three such big sillies as you three before; and now I shall start out on my travels again, and when I can find three bigger sillies than you three, then I'll come back and marry your daughter." So he wished them good-by, and started off on his travels, and left them all crying because the girl had lost her sweetheart.

Well, he set out, and he traveled a long way, and at last he came to a woman's cottage that had some grass growing on the roof. And the woman was trying to get her cow to go up a ladder to the grass, and the poor thing durst not go. So the gentleman asked the woman what she was doing. "Why, lookee," she said, "look at all that beautiful grass. I'm going to get the cow on to the roof to eat it.

She'll be quite safe, for I shall tie a string round her neck, and pass it down the chimney, and tie it to my wrist as I go about the house, so she can't fall off without my knowing it." "Oh, you poor silly!" said the gentleman, "you should cut the grass and throw it down to the cow!" But the woman thought it was easier to get the cow up the ladder than to get the grass down, so she pushed her and coaxed her and got her up, and tied a string round her neck, and passed it down the chimney, and fastened it to her own wrist. And the gentleman went on his way, but he hadn't gone far when the cow tumbled off the roof.

Well, that was one big silly.

And the gentleman went on and on, and he went to an inn to stop that night, and they were so full at the inn that they had to put him in a double-bedded room, and another traveler was to sleep in the other bed. The other man was a very pleasant fellow, and they got very friendly together; but in the morning, when they were both getting up, the gentleman was surprised to see the other hang his trousers on the knobs of the chest of drawers and run across the room and try to jump into them, and he tried over and over again, and couldn't manage it; and the gentleman wondered whatever he was doing it for. At last he stopped and wiped his face with his handkerchief.

     LumosTestPrep.com

Oh dear," he says, "I do think trousers are the most awkward kind of clothes that ever were. I can't think who could have invented such things. It takes me the best part of an hour to get into mine every morning, and I get so hot! How do you manage yours?" So the gentleman burst out laughing, and showed him how to put them on; and he was very much obliged to him, and said he never should have thought of doing it that way. So that was another big silly.

Then the gentleman went on his travels again; and he came to a village, and outside the village there was a pond, and round the pond was a crowd of people. And they had rakes, and brooms, and pitchforks, reaching into the pond; and the gentleman asked what the matter was. "Why," they say, "matter enough! Moon's tumbled into the pond, and we can't rake her out anyhow!"

So the gentleman burst out laughing, and told them to look up into the sky, and that it was only the shadow in the water. But they wouldn't listen to him, and shouted at him shamefully and he got away as quick as he could.

So there were a whole lot of sillies bigger than the three sillies at home. So the gentleman turned back home again and married the farmer's daughter, and if they didn't live happy forever after, but that's nothing to do with you or me.

     LumosTestPrep.com

1. Which of the following is the best possible word for mallet?

Ⓐ   Hammer
Ⓑ   House
Ⓒ   Lawn
Ⓓ   Liquid

2. What does the author describe as the first silly?

Ⓐ   the woman with the cow on the roof
Ⓑ   the three crying family members
Ⓒ   the man and his trousers
Ⓓ   none of these

3. What is the best possible adjective to describe the daughter of the story?

Ⓐ   emotional
Ⓑ   tough
Ⓒ   clever
Ⓓ   musical

4. What genre is the passage above?

Ⓐ   Science fiction
Ⓑ   Historical fiction
Ⓒ   Fairy tale
Ⓓ   Nonfiction

5. Based on the language in the story, when do you think this story was written? Choose the best possible answer.

Ⓐ   in the past 10 years
Ⓑ   in the past twenty years
Ⓒ   in the past 100 years
Ⓓ   300 years ago

6. According to the above passage what was the second silly trying to do?

Ⓐ   was crying in the wine cellar
Ⓑ   was coaxing the cow to go up on the roof and eat the over grown grass
Ⓒ   was trying to jump in to his trousers by hanging it on the dresser
Ⓓ   was trying to rake the moon out of the lake

7. How many sillies did the gentleman meet in all?

    Ⓐ 2 sillies
    Ⓑ 3 sillies
    Ⓒ 4 sillies
    Ⓓ 6 sillies

8. What adjective could be used to describe the gentleman?

    Ⓐ Smart
    Ⓑ Foolish
    Ⓒ Brave
    Ⓓ None of these

9. What is the summary of the above story?

    Ⓐ The world is filled only with smart people
    Ⓑ There are a lot more sillies in the world than you think
    Ⓒ The world is filled only with sillies
    Ⓓ There are a lot more smart people in the world than sillies

Here are some reminders for completing this Open-Ended task:

- Focus your response on the question asked.
- Answer all parts of the question and explain your answer with specific details.
- Use specific information from the story to answer all the parts of the question.

10. This story seems to be written many years ago.

- Discuss why you think the story took place many years ago.
- Describe what words in the story make you believe that the passage was written many years ago.
- Explain where you think the story took place.

LumosTestPrep.com

Writing Task 2
Directions to the Student

Read the poem "Try Again". After you are done, you will do a writing task. The poem may give you ideas for your writing.

Try Again

'Tis a lesson you should heed,
Try, try, try again;
If at first you don't succeed,
Try, try, try again.
Once or twice though you should fail
Try again;
If you would at last prevail,
Try again.
If we strive, 'tis no disgrace
Though we may not win the race;
What should you do in that case?
Try again.
If you find your task is hard,
Try again;
Time will bring you your reward,
Try again.
All that other folks can do,
With your patience should not you?
Only keep this rule in view—
Try again.
- Anonymous

Writing Task 2

After reading the poem, think of a time where you needed to continue trying until you accomplished something.
In a 3-paragraph essay, explain:

- **Discuss what you were trying to do**
- **Describe why you didn't think it was working**
- **Explain how you accomplished the task**

- You may take notes, create a web, or do other prewriting work. Then, write your composition on the lines provided.
- After you finish writing your composition, carefully read what you have written and make sure that your writing is the best it can be.

   LumosTestPrep.com

Prewriting Area

Writing Task 2

Reading Task 2
Directions to the Student

Now you will read another passage and answer the questions that follow. Some questions will be multiple-choice; others will be open-ended.

- You may look back at the reading passage as often as you want.
- Read each question carefully and think about the answer and fill in the circle completely next to your choice.
- If you do not know the answer to a question, go on to the next question and come back to the skipped question later.

LumosTestPrep.com

Trumpeter Swans
by Jodi-Anne Kaspin

For those of you who are E.B. White fans, who is the author of Charlotte's Web, you may have read or at least heard of the book, the Trumpet of the Swan. It's a story about a lovely swan

couple that gives birth to 5 little cygnets, and one of them isn't able to make the trumpeter sounds like a typical swan. Louis, the cygnet with special needs, searches to find a way communicate in other ways with his family and the swan he loves. The ending is yours to find out! But while reading the book, I'm sure many readers became curious about the trumpeter swans, which have a magical, beautiful aura about them. Read on to find out more these interesting creatures!

The Trumpeter Swans are the largest waterfowl. They weigh between 21-30 pounds, and males can even reach 35 pounds or more! While standing, they reach about four feet tall, about the size of the average second grader! Their wings span can reach up to eight feet long. It's difficult to imagine when the average person's arm span reaches six feet! The males are referred as cobs, and the females are known as pens. The Trumpeter Swans are known for their deep, loud calls that sound trumpet-like.

Trumpeter Swans can mate as early as three years old. However, most Trumpeters do not mate and nest until the ages of four to six. Trumpeters actually find a mate for life. Once they find their mate, they create a bond that lasts until the death of the first one. These birds can live, though, until thirty years of age! When one of the swans dies, the other usually finds another mate, usually younger. When "remating," the cob or pen usually returns to their former nesting area as long as they were successful at having several cygnets at that place.

Just like in the E.B. White novel, Trumpeter Swans were most often found in the northern United States, like Montana and Minnesota, and in Canada. Unfortunately, during the 1800s, swans were killed for their beautiful feathers and the population of the swans depleted. Trumpeters are known to enjoy forested areas and are most often found near swamps or shallow ponds. By 1900, it was believed that the Trumpeter Swans had become extinct. However, a few survived and were found in the valleys of Montana, Idaho, and Wyoming. By 1935, the United States government created the Red Rock Lakes National Wildlife Refuge to protect these creatures from becoming extinct. The government made the improvements to the habitats, provided food during the harsh northern United States winter conditions, and controlled hunting. Thanks to the Refuge, the Trumpeter Swan population has grown immensely and is no longer on the U.S. government endangered list. They can still be found in Montana, Idaho, and other midwestern states, and Canada. Today, there is even a huge population in Alaska, with more than 12,000 Trumpeter Swans choosing to reside there. If you decide to visit any of these areas, such as the Red Rocks Lakes in Montana, and hear a loud, deep pitched "ko-hoh" sound, you will now know that it could be the mating sound of these interesting breed of waterfowl that was saved from extinction.

11. Why do you think the author introduced the passage with The Trumpet of the Swan? Choose the best possible answer.

Ⓐ **To see how many readers actually read the story**
Ⓑ **To introduce the passage with a connection to the E.B. White story**
Ⓒ **The author's favorite author is E.B. White**
Ⓓ **The author enjoys reading about Trumpeter Swans**

12. What is the best possible explanation for the author writing this passage?

Ⓐ **The author probably likes to hunt Trumpeter Swans**
Ⓑ **The author probably works for the Red Rocks Lakes National Wildlife Refuge**
Ⓒ **The author most likely wanted the audience to learn more about Trumpeter Swans**
Ⓓ **The author most likely lives in the Midwestern United States**

13. Based on the passage, what kinds of habitat can a Trumpeter Swan most likely be found?

Ⓐ **near a swampy, forested area**
Ⓑ **flying in the air**
Ⓒ **at a zoo**
Ⓓ **in the plains of the Midwest**

14. Based on the information in the passage, how likely is it to find Trumpeter Swans in California or Nevada?

Ⓐ **Likely**
Ⓑ **Very Likely**
Ⓒ **Not Very Likely**
Ⓓ **None of these**

LumosTestPrep.com

15. **Which type of animal do you think has a mating practice similar to the Trumpeter Swan? Choose the best possible answer based on paragraph three in the passage.**

Ⓐ   **Humans**
Ⓑ   **Dogs**
Ⓒ   **Gorillas**
Ⓓ   **Fish**

16. **What would be an appropriate title for this passage?**

Ⓐ   **The Trumpeter Swans**
Ⓑ   **The Swans**
Ⓒ   **The Midwestern birds**
Ⓓ   **The Big birds**

17. **In the first paragraph, what does the word "aura" mean?**

Ⓐ   **Atmosphere**
Ⓑ   **Scent**
Ⓒ   **Water**
Ⓓ   **Charm**

18. **What are the male and female Swans called?**

Ⓐ   **Pens and Cygnets**
Ⓑ   **Cobs and Cygnets**
Ⓒ   **Pens and Cobs**
Ⓓ   **None of these**

19. **According to the above passage what is the name of the refuge that the USA government created to protect the Trumpeter Swans from becoming extinct?**

Ⓐ   **Pens and Cobs**
Ⓑ   **Cygnets**
Ⓒ   **Red Rocks Lakes**
Ⓓ   **None of these**

Here are some reminders for completing this Open-Ended task:

- Focus your response on the question asked.
- Answer all parts of the question and explain your answer with specific details.
- Use specific information from the story to answer all the parts of the question.

20. **The Trumpeter of the Swan, by E.B. White, which was written in 1970, made people aware of the Trumpeter Swans.**

- **Discuss whether or not you think the book affected the Trumpeter Swan population.**
- **Describe how you think the Trumpeter Swan population could have changed.**
- **Explain why you think the book affected the Trumpeter Swan population.**

Reading Task 3

Directions to the Student

Now you will read a story and answer the questions that follow.
Some questions will be multiple-choice; others will be open-ended.

- You may look back at the reading passage as often as you want.
- Read each question carefully and think about the answer and fill in the circle completely next to your choice.
- If you do not know the answer to a question, go on to the next question and come back to the skipped question later.

LumosTestPrep.com

The Civil War of the United States
by Jodi-Anne Kaspin

The Civil War of the United States, where the northern states and the southern states were at war with one another over slavery, was a time where almost all Americans had a loved one who was killed in the war. Men, and sometimes women, of all ages, were killed fighting for what they believed in. Right after the America Civil War ended in 1865, many American families wanted to remember those who had given their lives for their country. "Decoration Day," as it was originally called, was a day to celebrate and honor those who were lost during the war. Many people visited cemeteries of loves ones and "decorated" their graves with flowers, wreaths, and other mementos.

In 1868, three years after the war had ended, "Decoration Day" became official: May 30th would be the day to honor those veterans of the Civil War. New York was the first state to officially recognize the holiday in 1873. In 1890, all of the northern states began to recognize the holiday. However, the southern states refused to recognize Decoration Day since they decided to remember the Confederate soldiers on different days throughout the year.

You may wonder, when did the name "Memorial Day" come about? In 1882, the name was first used, but was not officially used by the country as a federal holiday until after World War II. In 1968, the American government moved Memorial Day from May 30th to the last Monday in May. Memorial Day was to honor those who fought not only in the Civil War, but in any war that Americans were involved in: World War I, World War II, Korean War, Vietnam War, and others.

Many Americans today observe Memorial Day by going to cemeteries and memorials, where they decorate graves of relatives. Flags are flown at half-staff from early in the morning until noon. Red, white, and blue are displayed on yards, parks, and around towns and cities. For many years, poppies, a colorful flower, were worn to commemorate this holiday. American flags are put up on lawns. Many Americans may attend parades or barbeques with friends and families. When walking down a street, one often smells the scent of hotdogs and hamburgers. The holiday is known by some to mark the beginning of summer. Beaches and pools are often opened on this day to celebrate the start of the hot season! Just like Memorial Day "opens" the summer season, Labor Day is known to "close" the season.

Memorial Day today is a federal holiday, which requires that businesses be closed in observance; so many Americans have a full three-day weekend. Although many events take place during this long weekend, it is said that many people forget the full reason of why Memorial Day is celebrated. As a result, a "Nation Moment of Remembrance" resolution was passed in December 2000, which asks Americans to devote 3:00 pm (Washington time) on that day to a moment to remember those who gave their lives for the United States.

21. Why was Memorial Day called "Decoration Day" after the Civil War?

Ⓐ Soldiers uniforms were decorated
Ⓑ Decoration were put up around towns
Ⓒ Graves of dead soldiers were decorated
Ⓓ None of the above

22. When was the holiday officially changed to "Memorial Day?"

Ⓐ 1868
Ⓑ 1873
Ⓒ After World War II
Ⓓ After the Civil War

23. Why was the holiday changed from "Decoration Day" to "Memorial Day?"

Ⓐ The article doesn't say why
Ⓑ Americans thought it was a nicer name
Ⓒ It had more to do with memorials than decorations
Ⓓ None of these answers

24. What are two things that were previously used to celebrate Memorial Day that no longer are used often?

Ⓐ It was called Decoration Day and flags were displayed
Ⓑ Poppies were worn and Decoration Day was celebrated
Ⓒ Americans celebrate exactly the same as they did after the Civil War and people have barbeques
Ⓓ All of the above

25. What is another federal holiday besides Memorial Day?

Ⓐ Christmas
Ⓑ Labor Day
Ⓒ July 4th
Ⓓ B & C

26. The Civil War ended in _____.

Ⓐ 1890
Ⓑ 1882
Ⓒ 1865
Ⓓ 1873

27. According to the above passage what was the reason for the Civil War?

- Ⓐ   Northern states
- Ⓑ   Southern states
- Ⓒ   Declaration Day
- Ⓓ   Slavery

28. Memorial Day opens summer season, _____ day closes the season.

- Ⓐ   Wintery
- Ⓑ   Labor
- Ⓒ   Memorial
- Ⓓ   July 4th

29. What was the resolution that was passed in December 2000?

- Ⓐ   Nation Moment of Remembrance
- Ⓑ   The Civil War of United States
- Ⓒ   Peace between northern and southern states
- Ⓓ   None of these

Here are some reminders for completing this Open-Ended task:

- Focus your response on the question asked.
- Answer all parts of the question and explain your answer with specific details.
- Use specific information from the story to answer all the parts of the question

30. The above passage talks about Memorial Day.

- **Discuss the importance of Memorial Day.**
- **Describe why you think that people seem to have forgotten the true reason for celebrating Memorial Day.**
- **Explain your answer above.**

End Of Practice Test 1

Sample Answer for Writing Task 1

A 5-point response should include:

- Answers to all parts of the question
- Reference to the text in the response
- Personal comparisons

    I've had many favorite authors, but my most favorite would probably be the author Franklin W. Dixon of the Hardy Boys. He has written almost 200 mystery books about the Hardy Boys and creates so much suspense in his stories. Every book makes you want to read more and leads you deeper into the mystery. I haven't known any other author who writes as greatly as him and has so much variety in his books! Really, if you get the chance to read his books, it is an amazing series!

    One of the reasons I enjoy reading his books is, because he creates suspense in his books. This keeps you at the edge of your seat waiting to see what happens next. Another reason why I like him so much is that he creates books with a mystery theme to them. Suspense and mystery go hand in hand with each other creating a whole new realm of adventure. Some people may enjoy mysteries and others may not. But to me, Dixon's books are something that everyone should enjoy. Finally, I like his stories because he tells the story from two boys' point of view who love to go on different adventures. Instead of using adults and say how their mind thinks, the author thought of a way to see how two boys would think. This made the story very exciting and fun to read.

    Out of all the books I've read so far from his series, "The Twisted Claw" was probably the best one. This book is about a series of museum thefts involving the smuggling of pirate loot. In the end, the Hardy Boys find out who was illegally taking the goods out of the country. But the book has all sorts of twists and turns to it while reading. You think one thing is going to happen, but the whole plot changes in a flash. And when you have the Hardy Boys, there is no telling what they will do next. Either it's hopping on to a dangerous ship or risking being captured to stop the thefts; they do it all. With the whole series, I think the author did a pretty great job building and transforming it into something wonderful and spectacular.

    I really think Franklin W. Dixon did an excellent job with his stories. He should get a round of applause for all the hard work and spirit that he has put into his creation. Not only has he created excitement in children's lives, but has let them see a new side of writing. When the word writing comes up, everyone starts moaning and groaning. But when the words come up saying that you have to write a mystery, all of that stops. The author has introduced a new world of literature to children when he first started writing his series. And he also expresses this in his writing. "It's okay to have fun writing!"

Reading Task 1 Answer Key

Question No.	Correct Answer
1	A
2	A
3	B
4	A
5	D
6	C
7	C
8	A
9	B

Sample Answer for Open – Ended 1

A 4-point response should include:

- Answers to all parts of the question
- Reference to the text in the response
- Personal comparisons

Based on the language in the story, I believe the story was written more than 300 years ago. One reason is because the story is about a farmer and his wife and many years ago, most people were farmers. There are few farmers today. Another reason is because the expressions in the story were used often many, many years ago. Some of these words and phrases are "drawing the juice," "courting" and "a-thinking." Today we would use the phrases, "I'm getting some juice," "they are dating," and "I was thinking." For these reasons, I believe the story was written more than 300 years ago.

Even though the story never mentions the setting, I believe it takes place in England since there is a lot of farmland there. The characters in the story speak with similar language that may be used by English characters in other books.

Sample Answer for Writing Task 2

A 5-point response should include:

- Answers to all parts of the question
- Reference to the text in the response
- Personal comparisons

I couldn't wait to ride my brand new bike. Once the training wheels were on it, I headed to the park every day with my dad to practice. We would practice for hours and hours until the sun would set. My dad and I did this for days. He would hold onto my bike as I rode and would yell, "Keep going! You can do it!" as I would pedal with all my might. After he would say this, he would let go of the bike and I always ended up falling on the ground. I thought I might never be able to ride on my own.

I decided to practice by myself when my dad wasn't home from work. I was determined to ride without an adult holding onto the back. I would sit on the bike and practice balancing first. Then I would slowly start to push the pedals and would begin to move. The next time my dad and I went out, we tried and I was able to do it. "You did it!" my dad shouted. This was the best moment of my life!

Reading Task 2 Answer Key

Question No.	Correct Answer
11	D
12	D
13	B
14	D
15	B
16	A
17	A
18	C
19	C

Sample Answer for Open - Ended 2

A 4-point response should include:

- Answers to all parts of the question
- Reference to the text in the response
- Personal comparisons

     I believe the Trumpeter Swan population was affected in a good way, thanks to the book, The Trumpeter of the Swan. I believe the population grew as a result. The book educated both children and adults about the Trumpeter Swans and I think that people grew attached to them after reading the book. When the book was written, people at that time may have had an influence on the government and as a result, they might have been able to help the Trumpeter Swans. With the government creating the Red Rock Lakes National Wildlife Refuge, the population of the Trumpeter Swans increased tremendously.

Reading Task 3 Answer Key

Question No.	Correct Answer
21	C
22	C
23	A
24	B
25	D
26	C
27	D
28	B
29	A

Sample Answer for Open - Ended 3

A 4-point response should include:

- Answers to all parts of the question
- Reference to the text in the response
- Personal comparisons

Memorial Day is a day when we remember those who fought and died for our county during past wars. As the passage explained, Memorial Day has gone from a day of remembering those who died fighting for our country to a day of picnics in the park. People seem to have forgotten the true reason we celebrate Memorial Day because of the time of year. Memorial Day takes place at the end of May, right before summer begins. During this time of year, the weather is sunny and warm and school is beginning to end. People want to spend time with their families and friends, especially since most people have the day off. This is why Memorial Day is a day of family, friends, and fun and is not a day of remembering those who have died.

Notes

Practice Test - 2

Student Name: Start Time:
Test Date: End Time:

Writing Task 1

You are at your friend's house for a slumber party. You have played a lot of games and even watched a spooky movie. Now it is time to go to sleep, and you go to the bathroom to brush your teeth. Suddenly there is a clicking noise and the bathroom door locks from the outside. Write a story about what happens next and how you get out of the bathroom.

- You may take notes, create a web, or do other prewriting work in the space provided. Then, write your story on the lines provided.
- After you complete writing your composition, read what all you have written. Make sure that your writing is the best it can be.

Prewriting Area

Writing Task 1

© Lumos Information Services 2009   LumosTestPrep.com

Reading Task 1

Directions to the Student

Now you will read a story and answer the questions that follow.
Some questions will be multiple-choice; others will be open-ended.

- You may look back at the reading passage as often as you want.
- Read each question carefully and think about the answer and fill in the circle completely next to your choice.
- If you do not know the answer to a question, go on to the next question and come back to the skipped question later.

LumosTestPrep.com

Johnny and the Golden Goose
by Jacob Grimm and Wilhelm Grimm

There was once a man who had three sons. Johnny, the youngest, was always looked upon as the simpleton of the family, and had very little kindness shown to him.

It happened one day that the eldest son was going out into the wood to cut fuel; and before he started, his mother gave him a slice of rich plum-cake and a flask of juice, so that he might not suffer from hunger or thirst.

Just as he reached the wood, he met a queer old man, dressed in gray who wished him "Good day," and begged for a piece of the young man's cake and a drink of juice.

But the greedy youth replied: "If I were to give you cake and wine, I should not have enough left for myself; so be off with you and leave me in peace."

Then he pushed the little man rudely on one side and went his way. He soon came to a likely-looking tree, and began to chop it down, but he made a false stroke, and instead of striking the tree he buried his axe in his own arm, and was obliged to hurry home as fast as he could to have the wound dressed. And this was what came of offending the little gray man!

The following day the second son set out to the wood, and his mother treated him just as she had done her eldest son—gave him a slice of cake and a flask of wine, in case he should feel hungry. The little gray man met him at the entrance to the wood, and begged for a share of his food, but the young man answered: "The more I give to you, the less I have for myself. Be off with you." Then he left the little gray man standing in the road, and went on his way. But it was not long before him, too, was punished; for the first stroke he aimed at a tree glanced aside and wounded his leg, so that he was obliged to be carried home.

Then said the Simpleton: "Father, let me go to the wood for once. I will bring you home plenty of fuel."

"Nonsense," answered the father. "Both your brothers have got into trouble, and it is not likely that I am going to trust you."

But Johnny would not give up the idea, and worried his father, till at last he said: "Very well, my son, have your own way. You shall learn by experience that I know better than you."

There was no rich cake for the simpleton of the family. His mother just gave him a little loaf of dough and a bottle of old juice.

No sooner did he reach the wood than the little gray man appeared.

"Give me a piece of your cake and a drink of your wine?" said he.

But the young man told him he had only a dough loaf and a bottle of old juice.

"Still," said he, "you are welcome to a share of the food, such as it is."

So the two sat down together; but when Johnny took his humble share from his pocket, what was his surprise to find it changed into the most delicious cake and juice. Then the young man and his guest made a hearty meal, and when it was ended the little gray man said:

"Because you have such a kind heart, and have willingly shared your food with me, I am going to reward you. Yonder stands an old tree: hew it down, and deep in the heart of the roots you will find something."

The old man then nodded kindly, and disappeared in a moment.

Johnny at once did as he had been told, and as soon as the tree fell he saw, sitting in the midst of the roots, a goose with feathers of purest gold. He lifted it carefully out, and carried it with him to the inn, where he meant to spend the night.

     LumosTestPrep.com

Now, the landlord had three daughters, and no sooner did they see the goose than they wanted to know what curious kind of bird it might be, for never before had they seen a fowl of any kind with feathers of pure gold. The eldest made up her mind to wait for a good opportunity and then pluck a feather for herself. So as soon as Johnny went out of the room she put out her hand and seized the wing of the goose, but what was her horror to find that she could not unclasp her fingers again, nor even move her hand from the golden goose!

Very soon the second sister came creeping into the room, meaning also to steal a feather; but no sooner did she touch her sister than she, too, was unable to draw her hand away. Lastly came the third, anxious to secure a feather before the goose's master returned.

"Go away! go away!" screamed her two sisters, but she could not understand why she should not help herself as well as the others. So she paid no heed to their cries, but came toward them and stretched out her hand to the goose.

In doing so she touched her second sister, and then, alas! She too, was held fast.

They pulled and tugged with might and main, but it was all of no use; they could not get away, and there they had to remain the whole night.

The next morning Johnny tucked the goose under his arm, and went on his way, never troubling himself about the three girls hanging on behind.

Then what a dance he led them: over hedges and ditches, highways and byways! Wherever he led they were bound to follow. Half way across a sunny meadow, they met the person, who was terribly shocked to see the three girls running after a young man.

"For shame!" he cried angrily, and seized the youngest by the hand to drag her away.

But no sooner did he touch her than the poor person was made fast too, and had to run behind the girls, whether he would or no.

On and on they ran, until at length they came into the country of a powerful King.

This King had an only daughter, who all her life had been so sad that no one had ever been able to make her laugh. So the King made a decree that the man who could bring a smile to his daughter's face should have her for his bride.

When Johnny heard what the King had promised, he at once made his way into the Princess's presence, and when she saw the goose, with the seven queer-looking companions hanging on behind, she burst into such a hearty fit of laughter that it was thought she would never be able to stop again.

Of course, the Simpleton claimed her as his bride, but the King did not fancy him for a son-in-law, so he made all sorts of excuses.

"You shall have her," said he, "if you can first bring me a man who can drink up a whole canister of juice."

Johnny at once remembered the little gray man, and, feeling sure that he would help him, he set out for the wood where he had first met him.

LumosTestPrep.com

When he reached the stump of the old tree, which he had himself chopped down, he noticed a man sitting beside it, with a face as gloomy as a rainy day.

Johnny asked politely what ailed him, and the man answered: "I suffer from a thirst I cannot quench. Cold water disagrees with me, and though I have, it is true, emptied a barrel of juice, it was no more to me than a single drop of water upon a hot stone."

You can think how pleased Johnny was to hear these words. He took the man to the King's cellar, where he seated himself before the huge barrels, and drank and drank till, at the end of the day, not a drop of juice was left.

Then Johnny claimed his bride, but the King could not make up his mind to give his daughter to person who went by such a name as "Simpleton."

So he made fresh excuses, and said that he would not give her up until the young man had found someone who could eat up a mountain of bread in a single day. So the young man had no choice but to set out once more for the wood. And again he found a man sitting beside the stump of the tree. He was very sad and hungry looking, and sat tightening the belt round his waist.

"I have eaten a whole oven full of bread," he said sadly, "but when one is as hungry as I am, such a meal only serves to make one more hungry still. I am so empty that if I did not tighten my belt I should die of hunger."

"You are the man for me!" said Johnny. "Follow me, and I will give you a meal that will satisfy even your hunger." He led the man into the courtyard of the King's palace, where all the meal in the kingdom had been collected together and mixed into an enormous mountain of bread. The man from the wood placed himself in front of it and began to eat, and before the day was over the mountain of bread had vanished.

A third time the Simpleton demanded his bride, but again the King found an excuse. "First bring me a ship that can sail both on land and sea, and then you shall wed the Princess," he said.

Johnny went straightway to the wood, where he met the little gray man with whom he had once shared his food.

"Good day," he said, nodding his wise little head. "So you've come to visit me again, eh? It was I, you know, who drank the juice and ate the bread for you, and now I will finish by giving you the wonderful ship which is to sail on either land or sea. All this I do for you because you were kind and good to me."

Then he gave him the ship, and when the King saw it he could find no further excuse.

So he gave the young man his daughter, and the pair was married that very day.

When the old King died, the Simpleton became King in his land and he and his wife lived happily ever after.

1. **What type of story is the passage above?**

   Ⓐ Realistic fiction
   Ⓑ Nonfiction
   Ⓒ Poetry
   Ⓓ Fiction

2. **Why was the Simpleton able to marry the princess? Choose the best possible answer.**

   Ⓐ He outsmarted the King
   Ⓑ He outsmarted his father
   Ⓒ He answered the riddles
   Ⓓ None of these

3. **What were the ways in which the Simpleton was able to win his "prize"?**

   Ⓐ He brought a ship
   Ⓑ He "ate" all the food
   Ⓒ He "drank" all the juice
   Ⓓ All of the above

4. **Who do you think the little gray man was?**

   Ⓐ He was an invisible man
   Ⓑ He was like a magician
   Ⓒ He was a very wealthy man
   Ⓓ He was a mean man

5. **What is a synonym for obliged?**

   Ⓐ Grateful
   Ⓑ Silly
   Ⓒ Selfish
   Ⓓ Kind

6. **How many brothers did Simpleton have?**

   Ⓐ Two younger brothers
   Ⓑ One older brother and one younger brother
   Ⓒ Two older brothers
   Ⓓ Three older brothers

         LumosTestPrep.com

7. "Because you have such a kind heart, and have willingly shared your food with me, I am going to reward you. Yonder stands an old tree: hew it down, and deep in the heart of the roots you will find something."
What is the meaning of the word "Yonder" in the above paragraph?

Ⓐ   Over there
Ⓑ   Over here
Ⓒ   Nowhere
Ⓓ   Where

8. What was the decree made by the King? Choose the most suitable answer.

Ⓐ   He who makes my daughter cry will win her for his bride
Ⓑ   He who can win my daughter in a battle can win her for his bride
Ⓒ   He who can make my daughter laugh can win her for his bride
Ⓓ   None of these

9. What were the three things that the king asked Johnny to do?

Ⓐ   Drink all the juice in the cellar, and bring a big ship
Ⓑ   Drink all the juice in the cellar, eat all the bread, and bring a big ship
Ⓒ   Eat all the bread, Make the princess laugh more and bring a big ship
Ⓓ   Marry the princess, become the king and bring a big ship

Here are some reminders for completing this Open-Ended task:

- Focus your response on the question asked.
- Answer all parts of the question and explain your answer with specific details.
- Use specific information from the story to answer all the parts of the question.

10. **The passage above is a story about a simpleton.**

- Discuss the simpleton's personality.
- Describe whether you think the Simpleton was very simple or very smart.
- Explain your answer above.

Writing Task 2

Directions to the Student

Read the poem "Twinkle Twinkle" to yourself. Afterwards, you will do a writing task. The poem may give you ideas for your writing.

Twinkle Twinkle

Twinkle, twinkle, little star;
How I wonder what you are!
Up above the world so high,
Like a diamond in the sky.

When the glorious sun is set,
When the grass with dew is wet,
Then you show your little light,
Twinkle, twinkle, all the night.

When the blazing sun is gone,
When he nothing shines upon,
Then you show your little light,
Twinkle, twinkle, all the night.

In the dark-blue sky you keep,
And often through my curtains peep;
For you never shut your eye
Till the sun is in the sky.

As your bright and tiny spark
Lights the traveler in the dark,
Though I know not what you are,
Twinkle, twinkle, little star!
--Jane Taylor and Ann Taylor

Writing Task 2

The poem above is a well known song among children.

- **Discuss a time when you wished for something.**
- **Describe if you could have anything in the world, what you would wish for.**
- **Explain why you would wish for the item above**.

- You may take notes, create a web, or do other prewriting work. Then, write your composition on the lines provided.
- After you finish writing your composition, carefully read what you have written and make sure that your writing is the best it can be.

Prewriting Area

Writing Task 2

LumosTestPrep.com

Reading Task 2

Directions to the Student

**Now you will read another passage and answer the questions that follow.
Some questions will be multiple-choice; others will be open-ended.**

- You may look back at the reading passage as often as you want.
- Read each question carefully and think about the answer and fill in the circle completely next to your choice.
- If you do not know the answer to a question, go on to the next question and come back to the skipped question later.

Beginning of Paul Revere's Ride
by Charles Morris

It was a day mighty in history, the birthday of the American Revolution; the opening event in the history of the United States of America, which has since grown to so enormous stature, and is perhaps destined to become the greatest nation upon the face of the earth. That midnight ride of Paul Revere was one of the turning points in the history of mankind.

It was night at Boston, the birth night of one of the leading events in the history of the world. The weather was balmy and clear. Most of the good citizens of the town were at their homes; many of them doubtless in their beds; for early hours were kept in those early days of our country's history. Yet many were abroad, and from certain streets of the town arose unwanted sounds, the steady tread of marching feet, and the occasional click of steel. It was the evening of April 18, 1775, and British troops were getting ready for their mission.

At the same hour, stood a strongly built and keen-eyed man, with his hand on the bridle of an impatiently waiting horse, his eyes fixed on a distant spire that rose like a shadow through the gloom of the night. Paul Revere was the name of this expectant patriot. He had just before crossed the Charles River in a small boat, rowing need fully through the darkness, for his route lay under the guns of a British man-of-war, the "Somerset," on whose deck, doubtless were watchful eyes on the lookout for midnight prowlers. Fortunately, the dark shadows, which lay upon the water, hid the solitary rower from view, and he reached the opposite shore unobserved. Here a swift horse had been provided for him, and he was bidden to be keenly on the alert, as a force of mounted British officers was on the road, which he might soon have to take.

And still the night moved on in its slow and silent course, while slumber locked the eyes of most of the worthy people of Boston town, and few of the patriots were afoot.
Paul Revere heedfully watched the secret movements of the British troops. He had to warn the people.

Suddenly a double gleam flashed from far off. No sooner had the light met his gaze than Paul Revere, with a glad cry of relief, sprang to his saddle, gave his uneasy horse the rein, and dashed away at a swinging pace, the hoof-beats of his horse sounding like the hammer-strokes of fate as he bore away on his vital errand.

11. What do you think was the goal of the author in the second paragraph of the passage? Choose the best possible answer.

Ⓐ **To describe to the audience in detail what the scene was like**
Ⓑ **To show what the main idea is**
Ⓒ **To describe that this is a nonfiction passage**
Ⓓ **None of these**

12. What does "slumber locked the eyes" mean?

Ⓐ **eyes were locked shut**
Ⓑ **people were sleeping**
Ⓒ **people had their eyes wide open**
Ⓓ **none of these**

13. Why did the author call the ride of Paul Revere "birth right of one of the leading events in the history of the world?"

Ⓐ   It was the first event of our country
Ⓑ   It lead to the beginning of the events that helped start our country
Ⓒ   It was the birth of George Washington
Ⓓ   None of these

14. What is a synonym for "vital?"

Ⓐ   extra
Ⓑ   sad
Ⓒ   important
Ⓓ   unimportant

15. What is the purpose of the passage?

Ⓐ   To talk about Boston in the 1770s
Ⓑ   To describe the Revolutionary War
Ⓒ   To explain George Washington's part in the independence of the US
Ⓓ   To explain Paul Revere's part in the independence of the US

16. What is the meaning of the word "enormous" in the first paragraph?

Ⓐ   huge
Ⓑ   tiny
Ⓒ   precious
Ⓓ   vicious

17. According to the above passage the American Revolution started on _____.

Ⓐ   April 17th 1775
Ⓑ   April 18th 1776
Ⓒ   April 18th 1775
Ⓓ   April 17th 1776

Suddenly a double gleam flashed from far off. No sooner had the light met his gaze than Paul Revere, with a glad cry of relief, sprang to his saddle, gave his uneasy horse the rein, and dashed away at a swinging pace, the hoof-beats of his horse sounding like the hammer-strokes of fate as he bore away on his vital errand.

18. What is the meaning of this paragraph?

   Ⓐ Paul Revere saw the double gleam and ran away
   Ⓑ Paul Revere cried after he saw the double gleam
   Ⓒ Paul Revere was waiting for the double gleam flash and then went home
   Ⓓ Paul Revere was waiting patiently for the sign of the double gleam and as soon as he saw it he started on his important errand.

19. Which of the following set of adjectives can be used to describe Paul Revere?

   Ⓐ strong and short
   Ⓑ determined and brave
   Ⓒ keen and intelligent
   Ⓓ all of the above

Here are some reminders for completing this Open-Ended task:

- Focus your response on the question asked.
- Answer all parts of the question and explain your answer with specific details.
- Use specific information from the story to answer all the parts of the question.

20. The passage above discusses Paul Revere's famous ride.

- **Discuss why Paul Revere's was important in history.**
- **Describe what a better title would be for this passage.**
- **Explain why you choose this title.**

LumosTestPrep.com

Reading Task 3
Directions to the Student

Now you will read a story and answer the questions that follow.
Some questions will be multiple-choice; others will be open-ended.

- You may look back at the reading passage as often as you want.
- Read each question carefully and think about the answer and fill in the circle completely next to your choice.
- If you do not know the answer to a question, go on to the next question and come back to the skipped question later.

Prewriting Area

LumosTestPrep.com

The Cunning Little Tailor

by Jacob Grimm and Wilhelm Grimm

Once upon a time, there was a princess who was extremely proud. If a prince came, she gave him some riddle to guess, and if he could not find it out, he was sent contemptuously away. She let it be made known also that whosoever solved her riddle should marry her, let him be who he might.

At length, therefore, three tailors fell in with each other, the two eldest of whom thought they had done so many dexterous bits of work successfully that they could not fail to succeed in this also; the third was a little useless land-louper, who did not even know his trade, but thought he must have some luck in this venture, for where else was it to come from? Then the two others said to him, "Just stay at home; you can't do so much with your little bit of understanding." The little tailor, however, did not let himself be discouraged, and said he had set his head to work about this for once, and he would manage well enough, and he went forth as if the whole world were his.

They all three announced themselves to the princess, and said she was to say her riddle to them, and that the right people were now come, who had understandings so fine that they could be threaded in a needle. Then said the princess, "I have two kinds of hair on my head, of what color is

it?" "If that be all," said the first, "it must be black and white, like the cloth which is called pepper and salt." The princess said, "Wrongly guessed; let the second answer." Then said the second, "If it be not black and white, then it is brown and red, like my father's company coat." "Wrongly guessed," said the princess, "let the third give the answer, for I see very well he knows it for certain."

Then the little tailor stepped boldly forth and said, "The princess has a silver and a golden hair on her head, and those are the two different colors." When the princess heard that, she turned pale and nearly fell down with terror, for the little tailor had guessed her riddle, and she had firmly believed that no man on earth could discover it. When her courage returned she said, "You have not won me yet; there is still something else that you must do. Below, in the stable is a bear with which you shall pass the night, and when I get up in the morning if you are still alive, you shall marry me."

She expected, however, she should thus get rid of the tailor, for the bear had never yet left any one alive who had fallen into his clutches. The little tailor did not let himself be frightened away, but was quite delighted, and said, "Boldly ventured is half won."

When therefore the evening came, our little tailor was taken down to the bear. The bear was about to set at the little fellow at once, and give him a hearty welcome with his paws: "Softly, softly," said the little tailor, "I will soon make you quiet." Then quite composedly, and as if he had not an anxiety in the world, he took some nuts out of his pocket, cracked them, and ate the kernels.

When the bear saw that, he was seized with a desire to have some nuts too. The tailor felt in his pockets, and reached him a handful; they were, however, not nuts, but pebbles. The bear put them in his mouth, but could get nothing out of them, let him bite as he would. "Eh!" thought he, "what a silly blockhead I am! I cannot even crack a nut!" and then he said to the tailor, "Here, crack me the nuts." "There, see what a silly fellow you are!" said the little tailor, "to have such a great mouth, and not be able to crack a small nut!" Then he took the pebble and nimbly put a nut in his mouth in the place of it, and crack, it was in two!

"I must try the thing again," said the bear; "when I watch you, I then think I ought to be able to do it too." So the tailor once more gave him a pebble, and the bear tried and tried to bite into it with all the strength of his body. But no one will imagine that he accomplished it. When that was over, the tailor took out a violin from beneath his coat, and played a piece of it to himself. When the bear heard the music, he could not help beginning to dance, and when he had danced a while, the thing pleased him so well that he said to the little tailor, "Is the fiddle heavy?" "Light enough for a child. Look, with the left hand I lay my fingers on it, and with the right I stroke it with the bow, and then it goes merrily, hop sa sa vivallalera!"

"So," said the bear; "fiddling is a thing I should like to understand too, that I might dance whenever I had a fancy. What do you think of that? "Will you give me lessons?" "With all my heart," said the tailor, "if you have a talent for it. But just let me see your claws, they are terribly long, I must cut thy nails a little." Then a vise was brought, and the bear put his claws in it, and the little tailor screwed it tight, and said, "Now wait until I come with the scissors," and he let the bear growl as he liked, and lay down in the corner on a bundle of straw, and fell asleep.

        LumosTestPrep.com

21. What do you think contemptuously means?

Ⓐ liking someone
Ⓑ not liking someone
Ⓒ feeling depressed
Ⓓ feeling excited

22. What is a synonym for clutches?

Ⓐ control
Ⓑ arms
Ⓒ hands
Ⓓ body

23. What is an antonym (opposite) for dexterous?

Ⓐ skilled
Ⓑ clumsy
Ⓒ sour
Ⓓ easy

24. What is one way the little tailor tricked the bear from eating him?

Ⓐ He cracked a "nut" with his teeth and exchanged it with a pebble
Ⓑ He pretended to be tough and frightful
Ⓒ He was really a bear hunter
Ⓓ His brothers helped him defeat the bear

25. Why do you think the princess added the additional task for the little tailor?

Ⓐ She didn't want to marry the little tailor
Ⓑ She wanted to marry one of his brothers
Ⓒ She was a very proud princess
Ⓓ Both A & C

26. Which of the following would be an appropriate title for the above passage?

Ⓐ The three tailors
Ⓑ The smart little tailor
Ⓒ The proud princess
Ⓓ None of the above

27. **What was the riddle that the princess asked the three tailors to solve?**

Ⓐ she wanted them to guess her favorite color
Ⓑ she wanted them to guess the name of her bear
Ⓒ she wanted them to guess how many toes she had
Ⓓ she wanted them to guess the two colors of her hair

28. **What were the two different colors of hair, the princess had?**

Ⓐ A gray hair and a red hair
Ⓑ A silver hair and a golden hair
Ⓒ A golden hair and a gray hair
Ⓓ A golden hair and a red hair

29. **What would be an appropriate ending for the above story?**

Ⓐ the princess sends the tailor away because she did not like him
Ⓑ the other two tailors felt jealous of the little tailor, so they harmed him
Ⓒ the princess did not agree to marry the tailor
Ⓓ the princess saw that the tailor had spent the night with the bear and admired him for that and got married to him

LumosTestPrep.com

Here are some reminders for completing this Open-Ended task:

- •Focus your response on the question asked.
- •Answer all parts of the question and explain your answer with specific details.
- •Use specific information from the story to answer all the parts of the question

30. **The above passage talks about a very smart tailor who tries to win the heart of a princess.**

- •**Discuss your own 1 paragraph ending to the fairy tale.**
- •**Describe how the characters felt.**
- •**Explain what will happen in the future.**

End Of Practice Test 2

© Lumos Information Services 2009   LumosTestPrep.com

Sample Answer for Writing Task 1

A 5-point response should include:

- Answers to all parts of the question
- Reference to the text in the response
- Personal comparisons

It was a Friday night and I had gone over to my best friend's house, his name was Jack and he had the creepiest bathroom I have ever seen. I was terrified that night when I walked in the bathroom to brush my teeth and change in to my p-jays. This is the story on what happened that Friday night.

I told Jack that I would be right back because I had to use the restroom and change my clothes. He said OK and said that he would need my help setting up the sleeping bags after I got back. I agreed and left for the creepy place. When I got in I took out my brushing utensils and started to apply the toothpaste when, click click click all over the bathroom. I thought it was Jack trying to play a trick on me but then I heard him yelp by the linen closet which was way on the other side of the house. He was probably pulling all the sleeping bags down. Then I heard the biggest click and tried to open the door so I could get out of the creepy place, but the door was locked and no one could get out of that bathroom. I tried to bang on that door but nothing happened. It was as if everything in the world was mute, no sound at all. Then I turned around and saw some kind of weird mist building up inside the bath. Then I screamed for Jack and Mrs. Parker, but still no one could hear me. Then I turned and I noticed that the mist higher than the rim of the bath tub!

I was so scared and ready to scream as loud as I have ever screamed in the whole life, the mist started to come towards my feet and I couldn't say a word out of fear. Then a strange looking body rose from the bathtub. It looked scared and blue. I was so scared that I had goose bumps all over me and I was shivering like nuts. Then the click click started again and the body started to walk to me and then I screamed so loud that it got scared and everything went right back to normal, Jack unlocked the door from the outside and I fell right back because I was leaning on the door. I was panting hard and Mrs. Parker came running from the kitchen with two cups of hot coco in her hand. I was breathless and she kept questioning me what happen what happen Steve, but I couldn't talk. Then Mrs. Parker suggested that I should go home for the night and I could call tomorrow. I nodded my head and made Jack get all my belongings that were in the bathroom.

My mother came around 12:00 A.M. to pick me up and then I left that place with one wave and had the worst feeling in my mind. My mother did the same thing Mrs. Parker did. She questioned me, what happened dear, what happened. I couldn't speak and I may not speak again, for that thing will be keeping from going into that bathroom ever again.

Reading Task 1 Answer Key

Question No.	Correct Answer
1	D
2	A
3	D
4	B
5	A
6	C
7	A
8	C
9	B

Sample Answer for Open – Ended 1

A 4-point response should include:

- Answers to all parts of the question
- Reference to the text in the response
- Personal comparisons

The Simpleton was a very eager and young man. He was determined and never gave up even though his brothers were not successful. I think the Simpleton was actually very smart rather than simple just like his name says. He was very nice to the old man and did what he was told by his father. In doing this, many good things came to him. By following directions from the old man, he was able to marry the woman of his dreams, and also gain a large ship. At the end of the story the lucky Simpleton even became king after the king died. Due to his actions, the Simpleton was much smarter than people thought.

     LumosTestPrep.com

Sample Answer for Writing Task 2

A 5-point response should include:

- Answers to all parts of the question
- Reference to the text in the response
- Personal comparisons

There was a time when my mom was very sick. During this time, I would wish for my mom to get better. She got very sick and the doctors did not know what was wrong with her. No one knew how long it would take for her to get better. I would wish every night for the doctors to find out what was happening with her.

When I look out my window at night, I sometimes make a wish on the first star I see. I like to think that anything is possible and if I wish and pray hard enough, some of my wishes may come true.

If I could have anything in the world, I would wish for good health for my family. Although there are many material things that I could wish for like a new ipod, a pool, or lots of toys, these items will not last me forever. My family is so much more important to me and they will be with me for a very long time. That is why I want them to be healthy because I love them very much.

Reading Task 2 Answer Key

Question No.	Correct Answer
11	A
12	B
13	B
14	C
15	D
16	A
17	C
18	D

Sample Answer for Open - Ended 2

A 4-point response should include:

- Answers to all parts of the question
- Reference to the text in the response
- Personal comparisons

Thanks to Paul Revere, the American colonists during the Revolutionary War were warned of the British attack and could defend themselves. A better title for this story is "Riding into the Night." Paul Revere began his ride in Boston on a clear spring night. He watched the British troops as they headed toward the colonists and was able to warn the colonists about their arrival before they were attacked. This all took place in the middle of the night, as most of the colonists were asleep peacefully in their beds. Due to everything that Paul Revere did, this is why I would pick this title.

Reading Task 3 Answer Key

Question No.	Correct Answer
1	D
2	A
3	D
4	B
5	A
6	C
7	A
8	C
9	B

Sample Answer for Open - Ended 3

A 5-point response should include:

- Answers to all parts of the question
- Reference to the text in the response
- Personal comparisons

The next morning, the princess woke up and decided to check on the little tailor who she thought must have been dead in the bear cage. "Oh I feel so bad, but there was no way I could have married him," she whispered to herself. As she crept down into the cage, she noticed the tailor sleeping peacefully near the bear. Shocked, the princess screamed. The tailor awoke and said, "Good morning my future wife. When shall we be married?" The princess felt surprisingly proud of this little tailor and knew that they would be married as soon as possible

Notes

    LumosTestPrep.com

Practice Test - 3

Student Name: Start Time:
Test Date: End Time:

Writing Task 1

Imagine that you could become a super hero who has the power to lift heavy objects and fly. Write a story explaining what you would do with your powers.

- You may take notes, create a web, or do other prewriting work in the space provided. Then, write your story on the lines provided.
- After you complete writing your composition, read what all you have written. Make sure that your writing is the best it can be.

Prewriting Area

LumosTestPrep.com

Writing Task 1

LumosTestPrep.com

Reading Task 1
Directions to the Student

Now you will read a story and answer the questions that follow.
Some questions will be multiple-choice; others will be open-ended.

- You may look back at the reading passage as often as you want.
- Read each question carefully and think about the answer and fill in the circle completely next to your choice.
- If you do not know the answer to a question, go on to the next question and come back to the skipped question later.

The Three Little Pigs
English Fairy Tale adopted by Joseph Jacobs

Once upon a time, when pigs could talk and no one had ever heard of bacon, there lived an old piggy mother with her three little sons. They had a very pleasant home in the middle of an oak forest, and were all just as happy as the day was long, until one sad year the acorn crop failed; then, indeed, poor Mrs. Piggy-wiggy often had hard work to make both ends meet.

One day she called her sons to her, and, with tears in her eyes, told them that she must send them out into the wide world to seek their fortune.She kissed them all round, and the three little pigs set out upon their travels, each taking a different road, and carrying a bundle slung on a stick across his shoulder.

The first little pig had not gone far before he met a man carrying a bundle of straw; so he said to him: "Please, man, give me that straw to build me a house?" The man was very good-natured, so he gave him the bundle of straw, and the little pig built a pretty little house with it. No sooner was it finished, and the little pig thinking of going to bed, than a wolf came along, knocked at the door, and said: "Little pig, little pig, let me come in."

But the little pig laughed softly, and answered: "No, no, by the hair of my chinny-chin-chin." So the wolf said…"Then I'll huff, and I'll puff, and I'll blow your house in."   So he huffed, and he puffed, and he blew his house in, and chased the little pig all around the house, but the little pig ran away.

The second little pig met a man with a bundle of furze (furze: very spiny and dense evergreen shrub), and said, "Good man, may I have some furze to build myself a house." The man gave him the furze, and the pig built himself a house. And then once more came the wolf, and he said, "Little pig, little pig, let me come in."

But the little pig answered: "Oh No, Oh no, not by the hair of my chiny-chin-chin." So the wolf said: "Then I'll puff, and I'll huff, and I'll blow your house in."

So he huffed, and he puffed, and he puffed and he huffed, and at last he blew the house in, and chased the little pig all around the house, but the little pig ran away.

          LumosTestPrep.com

Now, the third little pig met a man with a load of bricks and mortar, and he said: "Please, man, will you give me those bricks to build a house with?"

So the man gave him the bricks and mortar, and a little trowel as well, and the little pig built himself a nice strong little house. As soon as it was finished the wolf came to call, just as he had done to the other little pigs, and said: "Little pig, little pig, let me in!"

But the little pig answered: "No, no, by the hair of my chinny-chin-chin."

"Then," said the wolf, "I'll huff, and I'll puff, and I'll blow your house in."

Well, he huffed, and he puffed, and he puffed, and he huffed, and he huffed, and he puffed; but he could not get the house down. At last he had no breath left to huff and puff with, so he sat down outside the little pig's house and thought for awhile.

Presently he called out: "Little pig, I know where there is a nice field of turnips."

"Where?" said the little pig.

"Behind the farmer's house, three fields away, and if you will be ready tomorrow morning I will call for you, and we will go together and get some breakfast."

"Very well," said the little pig; "I will be sure to be ready. What time do you mean to start?"

"At six o'clock," replied the wolf.

Well, the wise little pig got up at five, scampered away to the field, and brought home a fine load of turnips before the wolf came. At six o'clock the wolf came to the little pig's house and said: "Little pig, are you ready?"

"Ready!" cried the little pig. "Why, I have been to the field and come back long ago, and now I am busy boiling a pot full of turnips for breakfast." The wolf was very angry indeed; but he made up his mind to catch the little pig somehow or other; so he told him that he knew where there was a nice apple tree.

"Where?" said the little pig. "Round the hill in the squire's orchard," the wolf said. "So if you will promise to play me no tricks, I will come for you tomorrow morning at five o'clock, and we will go there together and get some rosy-cheeked apples."

The next morning piggy got up at four o'clock and was off and away long before the wolf came. But the orchard was a long way off, and besides, he had the tree to climb, which is a difficult matter for a little pig, so that before the sack he had brought with him was quite filled he saw the wolf coming towards him.

He was dreadfully frightened, but he thought it better to put a good face on the matter, so when the wolf said: "Little pig, why are you here before me? Are they nice apples?" he replied at once: "Yes, very; I will throw down one for you to taste." So he picked an apple and threw it so far that whilst the wolf was running to fetch it he had time to jump down and scamper away home.

The next day the wolf came again, and told the little pig that there was going to be a fair in the town that afternoon, and asked him if he would go with him.

"Oh! Yes," said the pig, "I will go with pleasure. What time will you are ready to start?"

"At half-past three," said the wolf.

Of course, the little pig started long before the time, went to the fair, and bought a fine large butter-churn, and was trotting away with it on his back when he saw the wolf coming.

He did not know what to do, so he crept into the churn to hide, and by so doing started it rolling. Down the hill it went, rolling over and over, with the little pig squeaking inside.

The wolf could not think what the strange thing rolling down the hill could be; so he turned tail and ran away home in a fright without ever going to the fair at all. He went to the little pig's house to tell him how frightened he had been by a large round thing, which came rolling past him down the hill.

"Ha! Ha!" laughed the little pig; "so I frightened you, eh? I had been to the fair and bought a butter-churn; when I saw you I got inside it and rolled down the hill."

This made the wolf so angry that he declared that he would eat up the little pig, and that nothing should save him, for he would jump down the chimney.

But the clever little pig hung a pot full of water over the bottom of the chimney, and just as the wolf was coming down the chimney he took off the cover and in fell the wolf.

A wolf never troubled the little pig again.

 LumosTestPrep.com

1. What was the sequence of the houses built in the passage?

   Ⓐ   straw, furze, mortar
   Ⓑ   mortar, furze, and straw
   Ⓒ   string, mortar, and straw
   Ⓓ   none of these

2. What is an antonym for sternly?

   Ⓐ   seriously
   Ⓑ   cheerfully
   Ⓒ   appreciative
   Ⓓ   strictly

3. What is the main idea of the passage?

   Ⓐ   A wolf tries his hardest to trick three pigs
   Ⓑ   A wolf is eaten at the end
   Ⓒ   Two of the pigs had their houses blown down
   Ⓓ   Three pigs make their houses out of different material

4. What are the two best possible adjectives to describe the wolf?

   Ⓐ   cunning and evil
   Ⓑ   evil and silly
   Ⓒ   selfish and original
   Ⓓ   crazy and needy

5. What does the author want you to assume happened at the end?

   Ⓐ   the wolf pops out of the pot
   Ⓑ   the pig becomes rich
   Ⓒ   the wolf is dead
   Ⓓ   none of these

6. What is moral of the above story?

   Ⓐ   Never give up whatever happens
   Ⓑ   Be strong and think positive
   Ⓒ   Hard work always pays in the end
   Ⓓ   None of these

7. The first pig builds the house with a bundle of straw. What does this tell you about the first pig?

   Ⓐ The pig is very smart and hard working
   Ⓑ The pig is lazy and not that very smart
   Ⓒ The pig wants to spend more time eating
   Ⓓ None of these

8. Which of the following would be an appropriate set of adjectives to describe the third pig?

   Ⓐ Strong and dumb
   Ⓑ Wise and hard working
   Ⓒ Dumb and fat
   Ⓓ Lazy and sleepy

9. Why couldn't the wolf blow the third house down?

   Ⓐ because the house was too strong and well built by the pig
   Ⓑ because the wolf had become very weak
   Ⓒ because the wolf did not try hard enough
   Ⓓ none of these

Here are some reminders for completing this Open-Ended task:

- Focus your response on the question asked.
- Answer all parts of the question and explain your answer with specific details.
- Use specific information from the story to answer all the parts of the question

10. The above passage explains a well-known story of the Three Little Pigs.

- **Discuss another possible title for the story rather than "Three Little Pigs."**
- **Describe why you think this would be an appropriate title.**
- **Explain what happens at the end of the story.**

LumosTestPrep.com

Writing Task 2

Directions to the Student

Read the poem "The Violet". Afterwards, you will do a writing task. The poem may give you ideas for your writing.

The Violet

Down in a green and shady bed
A modest violet grew;
Its stalk was bent, it hung its head,
As if to hide from view.
And yet it was a lovely flower,
Its color bright and fair;
It might have graced a rosy bower
Instead of hiding there.
Yet there it was content to bloom,
In modest tints arrayed;
And they're diffused its sweet perfume
Within the silent shade.
Then let me to the valley go,
This pretty flower to see,
That I may also learn to grow
In sweet humility.
--Jane Taylor

Writing Task 2

The above passage explains a well-known story of the Three Little Pigs.

- **Discuss another possible title for the story rather than "Three Little Pigs."**
- **Describe why you think this would be an appropriate title.**
- **Explain what happens at the end of the story.**

- You may take notes, create a web, or do other prewriting work. Then, write your composition on the lines provided.
- After you finish writing your composition, carefully read what you have written and make sure that your writing is the best it can be.

    LumosTestPrep.com

Prewriting Area

Writing Task 2

Reading Task 2
Directions to the Student

Now you will read another passage and answer the questions that follow. Some questions will be multiple-choice; others will be open-ended.

- You may look back at the reading passage as often as you want.
- Read each question carefully and think about the answer and fill in the circle completely next to your choice.
- If you do not know the answer to a question, go on to the next question and come back to the skipped question later.

LumosTestPrep.com

Independence Day
by Jodi-Anne Kaspin

As Americans, we often think mainly of parades, food, barbeques, and fireworks when we hear "July 4th." It's a time where people are off from work and take the time to celebrate the holiday with family and friends. However, we tend to forget about the real reason that we are celebrating—the independence of the 13 colonies from Great Britain in 1776.

The celebration of our independence began only a year after the event, in 1777. On July 4th, thirteen guns were fired, large dinners were held, speeches and prayers were said, and even fireworks were used. The following year, George Washington celebrated with his soldiers and John Adams and Benjamin Franklin held dinners for politicians. From years on, and all the way up to the present, American citizens continue to celebrate this huge event outdoors. It is considered a federal holiday, which means that all postal services, schools, and workplaces are closed for commemoration. Politicians often make speeches mentioning such topics as liberty, freedom, and our founding fathers.

Today, the fireworks on July 4th are often displayed with patriotic songs, such as "America the Beautiful," "My Country 'Tis of Thee," "This Land is Your Land," and of course, "The Star Spangled Banner." "The Star Spangled Banner, written by Francis Scott Key in 1812 describing the American flag standing strong as "bombs were bursting through air," is often a theme song played throughout the day.

Although July 4th is a holiday celebrated throughout the country, there are some significant events held annually that bring out the patriotism of local Americans. For example, the town of Bristol, Rohde Island is known for having the longest Independence Day celebration. Then there's the Nathan's Hot Dog Eating Contest that began on July 4, 1916, to end an argument between immigrants on who was more patriotic. The event is still held in Coney Island, Brooklyn, and New York City. In addition, over 500,000 attend a free concert on the lawn of the Capitol building. It is called A Capitol Fourth and ends in fireworks. And finally, since 1959, NASCAR has held their annual Pepsi 400 on July 4th.

In a very unusual, spooky play of events, July 4th is also the anniversary of the deaths of two of the Presidents of the United States, Thomas Jefferson and John Adams. Coincidentally, they were the only two presidents to sign the Declaration of Independence on July 4, 1776. Even scarier is the fact that they both died on the exact same day, July 4, 1826, which happened to be the 50th anniversary of the signing of the Declaration.

In summary, July 4th, or Independence Day, is a holiday celebrated by Americans all over the country in similar ways. Citizens arrange barbeques, pool parties, parades, and fireworks displays to commemorate the independence of our nation. Some events are more notable than others, yet this federal holiday carries a lot of meaning and patriotism for millions of Americans.

11. What was the main idea of the passage?

    Ⓐ Why July 4th is a day of fireworks
    Ⓑ The Spooky Coincidences of July 4th
    Ⓒ Where the Hot Dog Eating Contest is held
    Ⓓ The ways Independence Day is celebrated in the US

12. What is the importance of Independence Day to Americans?

    Ⓐ There are Hotdog Eating Contests
    Ⓑ It celebrates the independence of the 13 colonies from Great Britain
    Ⓒ There are free concerts held at the Capitol Building
    Ⓓ Thomas Jefferson died on the 50th anniversary

13. What does the word "commemoration" mean in the passage?

    Ⓐ celebration
    Ⓑ hard work
    Ⓒ fireworks
    Ⓓ none of these

14. If you had to choose which paragraph did not completely belong based on the opening paragraph, which one would it be? Choose the best possible answer.

    Ⓐ Paragraph 2
    Ⓑ Paragraph 3
    Ⓒ Paragraph 4
    Ⓓ Paragraph 5

15. When did Independence Day begin its celebration?

    Ⓐ 1777
    Ⓑ 1778
    Ⓒ 1826
    Ⓓ 1916

16. According to the above passage how was the first Independence Day celebrated?

    Ⓐ Everybody had parties and danced all night.
    Ⓑ Thirteen guns were fired, large dinners were held, speeches and prayers were said and even fireworks were used.
    Ⓒ Barbecues and fireworks were held
    Ⓓ None of these

17. What are some of the main highlights of today's celebrations?

Ⓐ   Speeches and parades
Ⓑ   Parades and games
Ⓒ   Parades, food, barbecues and fireworks
Ⓓ   Nothing

18. What would be an appropriate title to the above passage?

Ⓐ   July 4th
Ⓑ   Independence Day
Ⓒ   Independence Day celebrations in the USA
Ⓓ   Freedom day

19. According to the above passage _____ was the 50th anniversary of signing the Declaration.

Ⓐ   July 4th 1977
Ⓑ   July 4th 1976
Ⓒ   July 4th 1826
Ⓓ   July 4th 1916

Here are some reminders for completing this Open-Ended task:

- Focus your response on the question asked.
- Answer all parts of the question and explain your answer with specific details.
- Use specific information from the story to answer all the parts of the question

20. The above story discusses why July 4th is celebrated in America.

- Discuss why July 4th is important.
- Describe how July 4th is celebrated.
- Explain why you think the Star Spangled Banner is an appropriate song to play on July 4th.

Reading Task 3

Directions to the Student

Now you will read a story and answer the questions that follow.
Some questions will be multiple-choice; others will be open-ended.

- You may look back at the reading passage as often as you want.
- Read each question carefully and think about the answer and fill in the circle completely next to your choice.
- If you do not know the answer to a question, go on to the next question and come back to the skipped question later.

Christopher Columbus
by David H. Montgomery

Christopher Columbus, the discoverer of America, was born at Genoa, a seaport of Italy, more than four hundred and fifty years ago. His father was a wool-comber. Christopher did not care to learn that trade, but wanted to become a sailor. Seeing the boy's strong liking for the sea, his father sent him to a school where he could learn geography, map drawing, and whatever else might help him to become some day the commander of a powerful vessel.

When he was fourteen, Columbus went to sea. In those days, the Mediterranean Sea swarmed with war-ships and pirates. Every sailor, no matter if he was but a boy, had to stand ready to fight his way from port to port.

In this exciting life, full of adventure and of danger, Columbus grew to manhood. The rough experiences he then had did much toward making him the brave, determined captain and explorer that he afterwards became, and how we know of him today.

According to some accounts, Columbus once had a desperate battle with a vessel off the coast of Portugal. The fight lasted; it is said, all day. At length, both vessels were found to be on fire. Columbus jumped from his blazing ship into the sea, and catching hold of a floating oar, managed, with its help, to swim to the shore, about six miles away!

He then went to the port of Lisbon. There he married the daughter of a famous sea captain. For a long time after his marriage, Columbus earned his living partly by drawing maps, which he sold to commanders of vessels visiting Lisbon, and partly by making voyages to Africa, Iceland, and other countries.

The maps, which Columbus made and sold, were very different from those we now have. At that time, not half of the world had been discovered. Europe, Asia, and a small part of Africa were the chief continents known. The maps of Columbus may have shown the earth shaped like a ball, but he supposed it to be much smaller than it really is. No one then had sailed round the globe. No one then knew what lands lay west of the broad Atlantic; for this reason we should look, on one of the maps drawn by Columbus, for the great continents of North and South America or for Australia or the Pacific Ocean. Not being discovered yet by explorers, they are nowhere to be seen.

While living in Lisbon, Columbus made up his mind to try to do what no other man, at that time, dared attempt—that was to cross the Atlantic Ocean. He thought that by doing so he could get directly to Asia and the Indies, which, he believed, were opposite Portugal and Spain. If successful, he could open up a very profitable trade with the rich countries of the East, from which spices and silk would be brought to Europe. The people of Europe could not reach those countries directly by ships, because they had not then found their way round the southern point of Africa. Columbus was too poor to fit out even a single ship to undertake such a voyage as he had planned. He asked the king of Portugal to furnish some money or vessels toward it, but he received no encouragement. At length he determined to go to Spain and see if he could get help there. On the southern coast of Spain there is a small port named Palos. Within sight of the village of Palos, and also within plain sight of the ocean, there was a convent—which is still standing—called the Convent of Saint Mary.

One morning a tall, fine-looking man, leading a little boy by the hand, knocked at the door of this convent and begged for a piece of bread and a cup of water for the child. The man was Columbus—whose wife was now dead—and the boy was his son.

It chanced that the guardian of the convent noticed Columbus standing at the door. He liked his appearance, and coming up, began to talk with him. Columbus frankly told him what he was trying to do. The guardian of the convent listened with great interest; then he gave him a letter to a friend who he thought would help him to lay his plans before Ferdinand and Isabella, the king and queen of Spain.

21. **Why do you think Columbus may have had a difficult time trying to achieve his goal of traveling?**

   Ⓐ He had a family at home
   Ⓑ He was too young to become the commander of ships
   Ⓒ He was not educated enough
   Ⓓ He did not have enough money to supply the ships

22. **What is a big difference between life in the 1400's and life today?**

   Ⓐ There were Kings and Queens around the world
   Ⓑ People with little money had difficulty obtaining things
   Ⓒ People went to school to learn geography
   Ⓓ There were people that wanted to discover new lands

23. **What was Columbus' occupation before he became an explorer?**

   Ⓐ geography teacher
   Ⓑ map-drawer
   Ⓒ commander
   Ⓓ ship builder

24. **Which of the continents is missing on the map above?**

   Ⓐ Australia
   Ⓑ North America
   Ⓒ Asia
   Ⓓ A & B

25. **What do you think will happen to Columbus based on this passage and what you know about the history of Christopher Columbus?**

   Ⓐ The King and Queen of Spain will refuse to support Columbus
   Ⓑ Christopher Columbus will be provided with the ships and supplies he needs
   Ⓒ Columbus will succeed in doing EXACTLY what he intends to do
   Ⓓ None of these answers

     LumosTestPrep.com

Every sailor, no matter if he was but a boy, had to stand ready to fight his way from port to port.

26. What is the meaning of the above sentence?

Ⓐ   If you were a boy you had to fight
Ⓑ   If you were a sailor and a boy, you need not fight
Ⓒ   If you were a sailor and a boy, you could escape without fighting
Ⓓ   If you were a sailor and a girl, you did not have to fight your way from port to port

27. Which were the continents that could be seen on the maps made and sold by Christopher Columbus?

Ⓐ   Europe and Asia
Ⓑ   North and South America
Ⓒ   All of Africa
Ⓓ   Europe, Asia and some parts of Africa

28. What is the main Idea of the above passage?

Ⓐ   Introduce old world sailing
Ⓑ   Introduce Columbus and his life
Ⓒ   Introduce map drawing
Ⓓ   None of these

When he was fourteen, Columbus went to sea. In those days, the Mediterranean Sea swarmed with war-ships and pirates.

29. What is the meaning of the word "swarmed" in the above sentence?

Ⓐ   Filled
Ⓑ   Empty
Ⓒ   Busy
Ⓓ   Tricked

30. The above passage describes the beginning of Christopher Columbus' travels.

- Discuss the actions Christopher Columbus will take in order to begin his journey.
- Describe the role of the King and Queen.
- Explain how you think Christopher Columbus will feel.

End Of Practice Test 3

LumosTestPrep.com

Sample Answer for Writing Task 1

A 5-point response should include:

- Answers to all parts of the question
- Reference to the text in the response
- Personal comparisons

If I were a super hero with abilities that will allow me to fly and lift heavy objects, that would be the best thing ever. I would use my powers for helpful reasons and not for anything other than that. If I had the power to be a super hero then the world would be a better place to live.

If I had the power to fly, the first thing I would use it for, would be to do the groceries for my mother. I would also run some other errands for other people in town that would need the help. I would ask for the money needed to get all of their shopping done and then ask for a one dollar tip which would help me but other things that I would want. I would also use my flying power to take myself to school. With a little kick in my super strength, I could take all of my friends as well. I would be like Superman to everyone in town and the entire world.

If I had super strength, I would use my powers to stop the war in Afghanistan or any other place in the world so that the world would live in peace. I would also use my special powers to pick up heavy objects in the store for my mother or any other valued customer that will need help at a store. I would be very lucky to be able to be a courteous boy and help many people. I would also get many complements from all of these people.

Being a super hero would be very nice and having the power to lift heavy objects and fly would be even better. I would always use my powers to do good to others and sometimes myself. Having special powers would mean that I would be the luckiest boy in the world.

Reading Task 1 Answer Key

Question No.	Correct Answer
1	A
2	B
3	A
4	A
5	C
6	C
7	B
8	B
9	A

Sample Answer for Open – Ended 1

A 4-point response should include:

- Answers to all parts of the question
- Reference to the text in the response
- Personal comparisons

"The Wolf Who Couldn't Win" would be another name for the story the "Three Little Pigs." This name would fit the story because at the end of the story, the wolf ends up getting tricked. He tries to trick the pigs by asking to enter into their homes. When they refuse to let him in, he then blows down their house. In the end, it seems like the wolf is going to trick the pigs and win, but the pigs are too smart for him. They end up letting the wolf sneak in the house through the chimney only to find a pot of boiling water waiting for him. The wolf dies in the pot and the pigs remain safe from the wolf.

Sample Answer for Writing Task 2

A 5-point response should include:

- Answers to all parts of the question
- Reference to the text in the response
- Personal comparisons

I have a family member who reminds me of the violet in the poem. My cousin Joyce is very shy and quiet. When we have family gatherings she rarely talks to anyone and just sits alone, watching everyone talk and laugh. Although she is so quiet and shy, she is such a beautiful person to me.

My cousin Joyce has so much to offer and she surprises me every time I see her. She respects everyone and is always there to help anyone in need. Whenever she sees that a family member needs guidance or assistance, she is right there helping them. She speaks very little to our family members, but her actions speak from her heart.

Reading Task 2 Answer Key

Question No.	Correct Answer
11	D
12	B
13	A
14	D
15	A
16	B
17	C
18	C
19	C

Sample Answer for Open - Ended 2

A 4-point response should include:

- Answers to all parts of the question
- Reference to the text in the response
- Personal comparisons

The Fourth of July celebrates the independence of our country from Great Britain and is such a notable day. July 4th is celebrated in different ways, such as parades, fireworks, and barbeques. The Star-Spangled Banner is an appropriate song to play on July 4th because it is a song that represents America. The Star-Spangled Banner is a patriotic song meant to show the bravery of those that fought for our country. There is such a history to the song and it is a tradition to play the song every year for many years. Since the Star-Spangled Banner was written on the day when we were fighting Great Britain, it is an appropriate song to play on July 4th.

Reading Task 3 Answer Key

Question No.	Correct Answer
21	B
22	C
23	A
24	C
25	A
26	D
27	D
28	B
29	A

Sample Answer for Open - Ended 3

A 4-point response should include:

- Answers to all parts of the question
- Reference to the text in the response
- Personal comparisons

I think that Christopher Columbus will go to Spain and ask the King and Queen for the money to buy ships. He will do this because he is eager to sail and learn more about new lands. I think he hopes that the King and Queen will want to learn more about the new lands. I think the King and Queen will offer Christopher Columbus the ships and the men he will need to help him on his journey since they support his trip. Christopher Columbus will be very thankful to the King and Queen. He will use these ships and sailors to sail around the world and explore the unknown.

Notes

About Online Workbooks

◆ When you buy this book, 1 year access to online workbooks included

◆ Access them anytime from a computer with an internet connection

◆ Adheres to New Jersey Core Curriculum Standards

◆ Includes progres report

◆ Instant feedback and self-paced

◆ Ability to review incorrect answers

◆ Parents and Teachers can assist in student's learning by reviweing their areas of difficulty

Course Name: NJ ASK Grade 4 Math Prep

Lesson Name:	Correct	Total	% Score	Incorrect
Introduction				
Diagnostic Test		3	0%	3
Number and Numerical Operations				
Workbook - Number Sense	2	10	20%	8
Workbook - Numerical Operations	2	25	8%	23
Workbook - Estimation	1	3	33%	2
Geometry and measurement				
Workbook - Geometric Properties		6	0%	6
Workbook - Transforming Shapes				
Workbook - Coordinate Geometry	1	3	33%	2
Workbook - Units of Measurement				
Workbook - Measuring Geometric Objects	3	10	30%	7
Patterns and algebra				
Workbook - Patterns	7	10	70%	3
Workbook - Functions and relationships				

LESSON NAME: Workbook - Geometric Properties
Elapsed Time: 01:19

Question No. 2
What type of motion is being modeled here?

Select right answer
◯ a translation
◯ a rotation 90° clockwise
◉ a rotation 90° counter-clockwise
◯ a reflection

[Previous question]   [Next question]

Report Name: Missed Questions
Student Name: Lisa Colbright
Cours Name: NJ ASK Grade 4 Math Prep
Lesson Name: Diagnostic Test

The faces on a number cube are labeled with the numbers 1 through 6. What is the probability of rolling a number greater than 4?

Answer Explanation

<u>(C)</u> On a standard number cube, there are six possible outcomes. Of those outcomes, 2 of them are greater than 4. Thus, the probability of rolling a number greater than 4 is "2 out of 6" or 2/6.

A)   1/6
B)   1/3
C) Correct Answer   2/6
D)   3/6

    LumosTestPrep.com

Made in the USA
Charleston, SC
25 September 2010